CREATING EFFECTIVE TRANSITIONS

CREATING EFFECTIVE TRANSITIONS

Moving from the Elementary Grades to Middle School

C. Thomas Potter II, Kevin S. Koett, and Carol J. Christian

ROWMAN & LITTLEFIELD
Lanham • Boulder • New York • London

Published by Rowman & Littlefield
An imprint of The Rowman & Littlefield Publishing Group, Inc.
4501 Forbes Boulevard, Suite 200, Lanham, Maryland 20706
www.rowman.com

Unit A, Whitacre Mews, 26-34 Stannary Street, London SE11 4AB

Copyright © 2018 by C. Thomas Potter II, Kevin S. Koett, and Carol J. Christian.

All rights reserved. No part of this book may be reproduced in any form or by any electronic or mechanical means, including information storage and retrieval systems, without written permission from the publisher, except by a reviewer who may quote passages in a review.

British Library Cataloguing in Publication Information Available

Library of Congress Cataloging-in-Publication Data

Names: Potter, C. Thomas, author.
Title: Creating effective transitions : moving from the elementary grades to middle school / C. Thomas Potter II, Kevin S. Koett, and Carol J. Christian.
Description: Lanham : Rowman & Littlefield, [2018] | Includes bibliographical references.
Identifiers: LCCN 2017061856 (print) | LCCN 2018011159 (ebook) | ISBN 9781475842692 (Electronic) | ISBN 9781475842678 (cloth : alk. paper) | ISBN 9781475842685 (pbk. : alk. paper)
Subjects: LCSH: Promotion (School)--Case studies. | Elementary school graduates--Case studies. | Middle school students--Case studies.
Classification: LCC LB3063 (ebook) | LCC LB3063 .P67 2018 (print) | DDC 371.2/83--dc23
LC record available at https://lccn.loc.gov/2017061856

∞ ™ The paper used in this publication meets the minimum requirements of American National Standard for Information Sciences Permanence of Paper for Printed Library Materials, ANSI/NISO Z39.48-1992.

Printed in the United States of America

CONTENTS

Preface vii
Introduction ix

1 The Plight of Ricky Wright 1
2 A Lost Ball in High Weeds 11
3 Becky's Story 23
4 Top Dog Effect 29
5 Afraid to Take a Chance 35
6 Self-Actualization 43
7 So Each May Learn 49
8 Sight Unseen 57
9 Trials and Tribulations 65
10 Words Can't Express 71
11 Slacker 79
12 Social Immaturity 85

About the Authors 93

PREFACE

As a former elementary school principal, when my fifth grader was entering middle school it became apparent on a personal level how little was done between the elementary and middle schools to prepare students for the transition.

Fearful, anxious, and *ill prepared* are words that describe an elementary school student leaving the safety of the single classroom with one teacher and entering the multiclassroom and multiteacher schedule at the middle school. Can I keep up? Will I be accepted? Will there be supports in place to help me if I begin to falter?

With each new building transition, as in the move from elementary to middle school, students often enter into a larger, more impersonal school setting. The cohesive and caring atmosphere that existed for elementary students, where teachers knew their students on a personal level, is often replaced by one in which students wander aimlessly in and out of classrooms and where communication among faculty is limited. It is here where students can become lost in the transition.

These young learners—who once loved coming to school, learning new things, and being active participants—may now elect to disengage and disconnect. The downward spiral begins here unless teachers and school leaders recognize the importance of developing transition activities that can help elementary students ease their fears in the move to the middle school.

The authors hope this book, written from the perspective of real-life stories of students' experiences during the transition, will move educators to change their practices and intentionally implement activites to aid students in this transition.

INTRODUCTION

This book focuses primarily on elementary to middle school transitions. *Creating Effective Transitions: Moving from the Elementary Grades to Middle School* is one in a series of three separate but interrelated books that share scenarios about the journey through schooling and the obstacles students face in each transition.

Elementary students up to this point in education have, for the most part, moved each year from one self-contained classroom to another. They might even move just across the hall from one grade and classroom to the next. Students are acquainted with the building and likely see the same faces daily. Each year seems like business as usual. It is comfortable and safe, filled with the same routines, and everything seems familiar to them.

Middle school is often drastically different. Students have five- to seven-period schedules each day, with five to seven different teachers. The faces are never the same in each class. The building is often larger, with multiple floors and wings jutting out in all directions. Managing all of this change poses its challenges.

Too many middle school professionals adopt the attitude that it is time for these students moving to the middle school to grow up; they should no longer be babied. It is true that each transition involves a letting go of some things in the process of moving toward self-actualization and becoming a mature individual. But to go from a nurturing atmosphere to one with little to no lifelines or anchors can cause many once-successful students to sink—and fast. Transition activities are just that: activities that help students adjust to the many changes that are occurring developmentally and as a result of the move to a new school.

The purpose of this work is twofold: first, to help educators and parents understand the roles they play in meeting the basic developmental needs of individual students during times of transition; and second, to help school leaders understand how critically important it is for organizations to create structured transition processes that support the growth and development of students in order to better ensure student success before, during, and after transition.

Transition success does not happen by chance. Schools must intentionally develop activities that make transition an easier experience for students. As students navigate through the K–12 and post-secondary schools, multiple transitions occur that include (but are not limited to) moving to different, unfamiliar school buildings and going from self-contained classrooms with one teacher to departmentalized schools with numerous teachers. Most building transitions require a move to a larger, more impersonal school environment. It is during these periods of transition that students can become lost in the shuffle as they move through multiple-period days, various teacher routines and expectations, more complex schedules, and increased academic rigor, all at a time of great growth and developmental change. Each of these transitions can pose barriers to student success.

Many students lack the support structures at school and at home that help ensure a seamless transition; they may become lost in transition. Often these students begin to experience failing grades and an increase in inappropriate behaviors. As a result of frustration, fear, and the inability to cope with the stress, many students are at increased risk of dropping out of school.

The research that served as the foundational structure for this book centers on transition research and Abraham Maslow's understanding of human growth and development. The literature in support of this research serves to assist educators and parents in understanding why it is important to intervene with a purposeful set of transition plans and activities that are intentionally developed to help students during the move from elementary school to middle school.

This book is both practitioner based and parent friendly. Using authentic, research-based scenarios that illustrate the barriers associated with the transitional moves students may experience, this work and its companion books can assist school organizations and institutions in working collectively to strategically develop district-wide and interagency (high school and college) transition plans to help students during these critical periods.

In understanding human growth and basic levels of human need, educators come to better understand the total child: physically, socially, emotionally, and intellectually. In this era of high-stakes accountability, educators must not lose sight of the need to reach out to students at a deeper, more basic level rather than merely teaching content. Educators and parents should remember the importance of the inner, human developmental needs of our students and should think about what schools can intentionally do to ensure successful transitions by implementing transition actives that prepare students for these moves.

Educators often study the theory of learning in college. It is our goal that in using real-life stories, we can bridge theory with practice while providing suggestions for interventions that can be strategically embedded in individualized transition plans.

I

THE PLIGHT OF RICKY WRIGHT

The transition from elementary to middle school is one of the toughest educational transitions that students make; therefore, it is paramount that school districts begin to acknowledge this and put into action transition plans designed to provide adequate support for their transitioning students. This is a time in elementary students' lives when their world is seemingly turned upside down as they go from self-contained, one-teacher classrooms to multiple teachers in larger, more impersonal school environments (Stoffner & Williamson, 2000).

This is a time when preadolescent children need the support of parents/guardians, teachers, and school counselors more than ever (Mac Iver, 1990), though they often push away any such efforts during these times of great growth, development, and change. Parents and school staff need to be prepared to help children navigate the challenges and turmoil that are a part of this transitional period.

VIGNETTE

During Ricky's fifth-grade year in elementary school, he was at the top of his class. He was voted Mr. Hometown Elementary by his peers. He was very much the outgoing, well-mannered, and well-behaved student teachers loved. He was a very personable child who exhibited a harmonious sense of compassion for others. Ricky loved school; as his mother once put it, "He just can't wait for that bus to stop down at the mouth of the holler to pack him off to that school."

Ricky came from a split home. His biological father was in prison and had terminated all parental rights. His mother was a hard worker with little education. Though she tried to keep food on the table for Ricky, his two sisters, and his younger brother, it was often a struggle for her. Ricky actually had two younger brothers: a half brother and a brother who shared the same mother and father as Ricky. His mother's poor taste in men only compounded the struggles at home for Ricky and his siblings as she met and quickly married another uneducated, morally questionable character who worked in the local hills as a logger and general laborer.

One morning Ricky's teachers came storming into the principal's office, outraged that the younger of Ricky's brothers—his half brother—had brought to school a pocketful of dollars to squander on trinkets and supplies at the annual book fair, while Ricky and the others seldom even had snack money.

Upon calling home to inquire about the unusual sum of money the younger one had brought to school, the mother said simply, "I told him not to take that damn money to school, that he'd lose it or get it took by somebody a lookin' for a free meal." The principal then asked, "So the money is his?" She replied, "Yep, it's his; his daddy gave it to 'im." When the principal pointed out that Ricky and the other siblings hardly ever had snack money, she replied, "Well that's cause they ain't got no daddy and Junior does."

Although Ricky could have been the poster child for the HP2 (high-performing/high-poverty) kids, he always smiled. His teachers seemed to gravitate toward him because he sought to please them, always complying with their wishes. Whenever they needed a go-to person to handle such tasks as returning the snack cart or transporting ticket sales to the front office, Ricky was their guy. He was trustworthy and very dependable, and he had many friends throughout the building.

When Ricky began middle school in August of his sixth-grade year, life as he had known it all but ceased to exist. Four elementary schools were feeder schools to the middle school, and Ricky's peer group increased from thirty-four students in grade five to more than 220 students in grade six.

Ricky had always been in a self-contained classroom with only one teacher; suddenly he found himself assigned to six different teachers on a team with 220 other students. Though his fifth-grade teacher, Mrs. Watkins, frequently attempted to communicate with some of Ricky's new middle school teachers, more often than not she was met with disappointment as phone calls were not returned and e-mails went unanswered.

Ricky's former principal at Hometown Elementary school couldn't help but reflect on Ricky's time at his elementary school. He began to question if the school had made too much of a fuss over him, always ensuring that he had everything he needed for school, such as day-to-day supplies, paper and pencils, notebooks, and other necessities.

Had the school prepared him or crippled him in the transition to the middle school? Teachers often took money out of their own pockets to ensure that he had snacks or supplies. On more than one occasion the family resource coordinator had provided him with new clothing from local discount stores as she secured sponsorship for Ricky and his siblings. The staff of Hometown Elementary had assumed the role of surrogate parent for this child.

In October of Ricky's first year at the middle school, his former elementary principal ran into his mother at a basketball game and asked about Ricky and how he was doing. She informed the principal that Ricky was depressed; he hated school and he was failing. She indicated that he was not doing well at making new friends and that all of his elementary friends were in different homerooms. Ricky had commented that he never saw any of them.

She shared that Ricky was experiencing uncontrollable bouts of crying and did not want to go to school anymore. She said he repeatedly shunned her requests to discuss his issues and that he refused to do his homework. She indicated that the harder she tried, the more distant he became. She further shared Ricky once lashed out at her because she couldn't afford to buy him new clothes like the other students wore. He also had indicated that he felt like an outcast and that his tattered hand-me-downs made him feel different in a negative way.

The principal's heart sank as he stood listening to Ricky's mother talk about his struggles. He felt a sense of guilt at not having done more to help Ricky transition successfully to the middle school. The principal questioned what he had done and what he had not done. At that moment, the elementary principal realized that the system had failed this child.

Ricky's plight illustrates the powerful impact that social influences—a sense of belonging and fitting in with peers—have on transition success. For Ricky and many others like him, the effects of poverty combined with the challenges that come with transitioning to a new school have a negative impact on academic performance. Multiple teachers, differing teacher expectations, keeping up with various teachers' routines, and a new awareness of social class seemed to be too much for Ricky.

Ricky had come from a school where the teachers knew him. They were familiar with his family situation and the many barriers that are often the result of a life of poverty. Compared to elementary school, middle school—where he was just a number—seemed destined to produce circumstances where Ricky would become lost in the crowd and to fall through the cracks.

At the new middle school, Ricky realized for the first time that he did not quite dress like the others, that he had less than the other students. It was at the middle school that Ricky realized he was poor. He was subjected to the world of middle school fashion, dominated by brand names such as Hollister, Aéropostale, American Eagle, and Abercrombie & Fitch, to name a few.

This was Ricky's first exposure to the world of the haves and have-nots. He noticed for the first time that he did not have the trendy, expensive clothes that many of his classmates wore. He became preoccupied with wanting to fit in and quickly blamed his family's financial situation for his lack of the personal items required for entry into the "in crowd."

At the middle school, Ricky was on unfamiliar ground, and without a support net like the one the staff and resource center had provided at his elementary school, his chances for success were threatened. Nobody played mother hen for him, giving him the support he needed. Middle school teachers did not provide Ricky with gift boxes of clothing or backpacks full of paper and pencils, nor did anyone ensure that he had snack money. It appeared that his elementary school's approach for ensuring his success was not one the new middle school believed in. Ricky was ultimately fed to the wolves.

As Ricky's self-esteem plummeted—with nobody around to pick him up and put him back on track—he became increasingly withdrawn as despair took hold. Ricky's future was headed down the drain, along with his hopes and dreams.

Unfortunately, Ricky's plight occurs daily in schools across the country. School districts boast that "it's all about kids," when perhaps what they really should be saying is that "it's all about *all* kids." No child should be left to navigate this treacherous transition to a new school environment without a support networks of teachers who work collaboratively to create an environment conducive to student success.

RESEARCH

> During the middle grades, students in high-poverty environments are either launched on the path towards high school graduation or are knocked off-track. (Balfanz, 2009, p.13)

Transition researchers Hertzog and Morgan (1998) note that a well-planned and systematic approach in the transition from elementary school to middle school is paramount to the overall success of students. Research indicates that "schools with extensive transition programs have significantly lower dropout and failure rates than schools that ignore these important stages" (p. 96). These transition programs include activities that assist in the transition process, such as counseling opportunities for students and parents, school visits, and special summer courses aimed at allowing students to acclimate to and identify with the new school's culture.

The Kentucky Department of Education (n.d.) reminds us that schools that pay attention to transitions and schools that have an intentional transition plan see more success in increasing achievement and reducing retentions. Stoffner and Williamson (2002) acknowledge the importance of sound transition programs aimed at assisting transitioning students to enter "their new school confident and knowledgeable" (p. 48).

According to research of Midgley and Maehr (1998), schools and districts that focus on developing strong interpersonal relationships among their students and staff greatly increase the sense of school belonging. This, in turn, reduces the detrimental effects of negative attitudes about school, low self-esteem, self-deprecation, and feelings of anger. Schools must implement transition plans combined with support structures that provide students fair and equitable learning opportunities if "all students"—including those like Ricky—are to have a fighting chance.

INTERVENTIONS

Schools need to have transition plans in place that focus on the physical, emotional, academic, and social needs of elementary students moving to the middle school. Many school districts tend to focus only on the academic and procedural issues of transition, failing to acknowledge perhaps the most critical part: the social and emotional issues (Diemert, 1992).

As students move from the self-contained classroom setting of the elementary level to the departmentalized class schedules of the middle school, they need an abundance of ongoing support and assistance to navigate this often stressful transition (Stoffner & Williamson, 2000). A key element in assuring students this ongoing support and assistance before, during, and after the transition is adequate counseling and support by school staff (Stoffner & Williamson, 2000).

Strategies and Suggestions

The following intervention strategies and suggestions were developed from the research of Stoffner and Williamson (2000); Akos, Creamer, and Masina (2004); and Campbell and Jacobson (2008).

For teachers:

- Prepare both students and parents for the transition from the elementary school to the middle school:

  - Organize a parent orientation to review schedules and procedures.
  - Organize a student orientation to familiarize students with the building, rules, and expectations of the middle school.
  - During the orientation, allow students to move through their daily routines/class schedules for the upcoming year.

- Initiate student handoff programs designed to bring teachers and staff from both the incoming and receiving schools together to focus on meeting the needs of every child.
- Provide direct communication with parents of transitioning students:

  - Host a parent night at the school site prior to the start of classes.
  - Encourage parents to utilize school and district websites to acquire information pertaining to upcoming events.
  - Involve PTO organizations in transition activities, including membership drives to enlist new parents, sharing PTO newsletters, and preparing handouts for parents about fund-

raising information and educational opportunities for their children.

- Develop school newsletters notifying parents of summer transitioning events such as Jump Start programs, middle school open house events, and building tours for parents and incoming students.
- Develop peer mentor programs that allow older students to directly communicate with transitioning students.
- Plan school site visits the year prior to transition.
- Encourage middle school counselors to visit the elementary school prior to the transition to discuss the middle school's curriculum, homework policies, and social events.
- Develop adult mentor programs to acquaint incoming students with the middle school staff.
- Develop effective transition plans that focus on

    - increasing the communication between elementary and middle school teachers;
    - involving parents in the transition process; and
    - identifying the physical, emotional, academic, and social needs of the individual students.

For parents:

- Be actively engaged with your child's new school:

    - Attend orientation meetings.
    - Attend parent teacher conferences.
    - Join the middle school PTO.
    - Consider becoming a school volunteer.

- Arrange an appointment with your child's guidance counselor and teachers at the middle school as early as possible:

    - Be proactive and establish early dialogue with teachers, administrators, and staff.

- Communicate with other parents.
- Consider developing a support group for parents.

- Research and review literature pertaining to educational transitions:

  - Increase your knowledge of adolescent development.
  - Take time to review information and materials that relate to middle level issues.

- Review school policy and procedure prior to the start of school:

  - Lead discussions with your child about policies and procedures.
  - Attend site-based decision making (SBDM) council meetings at school.

REFERENCES

Akos, P., Creamer, V.L., & Masina, P. (2004). Connectedness and belonging through middle school orientation. *Middle School Journal*, *36*(1), 1–9.

Balfanz, R. (2009). Putting middle grades students on the graduation path: A policy and practice brief, p. 13. National Middle School Association. https://www.amle.org/portals/0/pdf/articles/policy_brief_balfanz.pdf.

Campbell, M.B. & Jacobson, M. (2008). From survive to thrive: The importance of transition. *Middle Ground*, *11*(3), 10–12.

Diemert, A. (1992). *A needs assessment of fifth grade students in a middle school.* Acton, MA: Author. (ED 362 332)

Hertzog, C.J. & Morgan, P.L. (1998). Breaking the barriers between middle school and high school: Developing a transition team for student success. *NASSP Bulletin*, *82*(597), 94–98.

Kentucky Department of Education. (n.d.) http://education.ky.gov. (Link to specific page is no longer active.)

Mac Iver, D.J. (1990). Meeting the needs of young adolescents: Advisory groups, interdisciplinary teaching teams, and school transition programs. *Phi Delta Kappan*, *71*, 458–464.

Midgley, C. & Maehr, M.L. (1998). *The Michigan middle school study: Report to participating schools and districts.* Ann Arbor, MI: Combined Program in Education and Psychology, University of Michigan.

Stoffner, M.F. & Williamson, R.D. (2000). Facilitating student transition into middle school. *Middle School Journal*, *31*(4), 47–52.

2

A LOST BALL IN HIGH WEEDS

For most students, leaving elementary school and moving on to middle school is just another experience on the journey through an educational career. For some, however, this transition—a rather significant milestone—brings about feelings of great anxiety.

In late spring of each school year, many elementary teachers and principals across the country stand before departing students during the fifth grade promotion ceremony. These ceremonies are intended to honor student achievement and commemorate what is hoped to be the first of many key educational attainments. Educators reassure students that transitions are simply changes, and that change is merely a part of living . . . and then we let them go.

It is quite common for transitioning students to have fears and concerns about the changes ahead and about what to expect at the next level. The minds of students in many intermediate classrooms across the country are consumed with the social issues that are a part of this transition. Students are often concerned about making new friends, fitting in, being safe from harassment, and being able to survive middle school life in general.

It is not uncommon to hear stories from students who feel safe and secure in elementary school but fear the move to the often larger environment of middle school. These students experience anxiety at the thought of leaving a place where everybody knows *their name and entering a place where they are likely to be just a number, where no one remembers their name.*

If educators know what students feel and fear during this transition, why do we not have activities in place to lessen these fears? How can educators and parents stop the negative effects—the sense of becoming lost in transition—associated with move from one school to the next?

VIGNETTE

In the spring before David was enrolled in kindergarten, the family resource coordinator and principal worked tirelessly to register local children for the coming fall's kindergarten class. It was during this time that the principal first met David and his mother, Rita. David was a small-framed, bright-eyed child with a hint of mischief in his demeanor. His inquisitive nature and fond attraction to anything in the wild that crawled, hopped, or slithered made him unforgettable to nearly everyone who knew him.

David lived with his mother, who had very little formal education and was, for all intents and purposes, illiterate. They lived in a dilapidated, run-down trailer at the head of a hollow where part of the road to his home was the creek bed. On numerous occasions when the weather was bad or the rain was heavy, David was not at school because he could not get out to the main road to catch the bus. His principal indicated that David's living conditions were subpar, perhaps the worst of any child in school.

As a school administrator in rural eastern Kentucky, in a district with an annual free and reduced lunch rate of 85 percent or higher each year, the principal had seen some pretty poor living conditions. To say that David's living conditions were some of the worst he had ever seen spoke volumes about the deplorable conditions this child endured.

In spite of of the senseless shootings in schools from Kentucky to Virginia to Connecticut over the past twenty years, school is still a safe place for children (Dinkes, Kemp, & Baum, 2009). For parents who daily live in survival mode, however, there are questions that need to be answered before they will allow their children to attend school. Educators often say parents who choose to keep their children at home are ignorant; perhaps those educators have never taken the time to get at the root cause of "stay-at-home kids."

David's mom lived in constant turmoil brought on by a nasty divorce. The Family Resource Center had worked with David and his mother to get him enrolled in kindergarten. It took quite a bit of prodding to convince Rita that her son would not be snatched from school by his estranged father, whom David had never met. The school reassured Rita that David would be safe, and that nobody could sign him out without her permission. The school gave her a tour of the building, pointing out the safety procedures the school enforces and the process for checking a child out of school.

Somewhat assured but still uncertain, Rita was in tears on the first day of school as she stood beside the double doors of the gymnasium while the new kindergarteners marched off to their classroom. Rita called out down the hallway in a piercing voice, "Don't lose David!" The principal quickly returned to her and gave her his word that David would be fine, once again promising her that nobody would take him. Rita wanted her son to learn and get a good education; she just needed reassurance that he would come home safely to her each night. Rita's inability to read and write never diminished her ability to love and care for her son.

When he reached middle school, David, like all adolescents, wanted to fit in at his new school. He wanted to be noticed for something positive to hang his hat on. Through his years in elementary school David had been nurtured by his teachers, each of whom seemed determined to strip him of his legacy of illiteracy. When David was in first grade, his teacher, Mrs. Deaton, asked the principal to come to her room to listen to David read. It was then that David was nicknamed "The Reading Machine."

It became a common goal of David's teachers to pay particular attention to this youngster. David's teachers not only wanted him to read well, but they wanted him to be the first in his family to graduate high school. By the end of fifth grade, the elementary teachers were steadfast in the belief that they had given David a strong foundation to go forth, be successful, and ultimately graduate.

As David entered middle school, his interest in school began to fade. By the end of the first grading period, he was failing and his problems were beginning to manifest. He ate alone in the cafeteria; he had no friends, and he appeared to be a misfit to the few who knew him by name. Few of his middle school teachers could put a face with his name when the elementary teachers inquired about his progress. When his former teachers periodically attempted to touch base with his middle school teachers to see how he was doing, they were discouraged by the lack of follow-up; the middle school teachers did not return their calls.

It seemed as though David had washed up on a desert island, lost and alone, with no provisions or support. When one of David's former teachers ran into his mom, to her dismay Rita told the teacher, "Well, David just don't like school no more. He does not trust those middle school teachers and they don't seem very willing to help him."

Rita also shared that she attended a team meeting only to feel like she too was being put down: "They used all of these highfalutin words . . . they made me feel so dumb. I can relate to what David must feel, if that is the way they are." The reason for Rita's disconnect with the staff was heard loud and clear when she said, "Them teachers over there think they are better than everyone."

As David continued his downward spiral, he was consumed with feelings of inadequacy and despair. He became increasingly critical of himself and his surroundings. In addition, he felt that he was constantly being compared to his peers in how they dressed, the clubs they were in, where they lived, and the talents they showcased. David once felt good about his ability in reading, but who cared about reading at the middle school? He began to focus more and more on his inability to fit in, both academically and socially.

He frequently made comments such as "The other kids are smarter than I am," "Nobody cares what I think," or "My teachers think I am stupid." What David needed most was a support structure much like the one in his old elementary school. He needed an intervention plan to assist him with his transition to middle school. He needed a teacher to connect with him, and his mother needed guidance as well on how to provide support for David at home. Without these transition supports, David was on a crash course toward becoming a high school dropout.

RESEARCH

Research by the American Educational Research Association (AERA, 2010) noted that schools are safer than the streets in many of the communities in which students live, and that violent crimes in schools have been on the decline since the 1990s. The AERA also notes that the most common form of violence at school comes from bullying and disruptive behavior.

According to the National Middle School Association (NMSA, 2006),

> Sometimes schools unwittingly erect barriers to family involvement by failing to recognize how intimidated many parents feel in settings where they did not achieve success during their own adolescence. Language difficulties, economic disparities, and work responsibilities can cause further estrangements. But other times schools and school districts actively discourage parents' participation such as focusing only on negative, one-way communications with families or excluding low-income and minority parents and guardians from important decisions that affect their children's education. By contrast, educators who strengthen home/school connections not only accelerate students' learning and development, they build support for middle level reform. (p. 27)

The NMSA research suggests that strong transition programs at the middle level can reduce dropout rates and increase retention rates by engaging parents and keeping families involved in their children's education throughout high school, leading to higher student achievement.

According to Midgley and Maehr (1998), middle schools that overemphasize the relative ability of their students tend to create negative outcomes for many students transitioning from elementary schools. The emphasis on relative ability in the classroom causes early and preadolescent children to develop negative attitudes toward school, becoming less likely to ask for help and more likely to create excuses for not completing assignments or engaging in discussion during class.

This research concludes that preadolescent students are naturally overly concerned with how they compare with their peers, and that when schools emphasize this comparison in the classroom it can be detrimental to students' academic progress. Schools that focus on relative ability rather than individual effort create a host of less-than-desirable outcomes. The good news is that when schools focus less on students' relative abilities and place more emphasis on effort and attitude, they create a positive or growth mind-set for students.

INTERVENTIONS

Children like David require effective transition plans combined with numerous articulation activities before, during, and after the transition. Many educators ask: Where do we start? How does one create a plan for a child such as this? One answer comes from St. Francis of Assisi: "Start by doing what's necessary; then do what's possible; and suddenly you are doing the impossible."

A joint paper by the National Middle School Association and the National Association of Elementary School Principals (2002) notes that the leadership, faculty, and staff of elementary and middle schools should work together to address students' concerns and to ease the transition to middle school.

Strategies and Suggestions

The following transition ideas and activities for leaders, teachers, counselor and parents come from a joint position paper adopted by the National Middle School Association and the National Association of Elementary School Principals (NMSA & NAESP, 2002) and personal experience.

For sending and receiving schools:

- Employ a "transition coach" such as a counselor or other staff member designated to track students' social interaction with peer groups as they transition to middle school. Transition coaches

   - work with students to reduce barriers and ensure that they are involved in extracurricular activities and events at school;
   - assist students in making new friends;
   - track student progress and support academic goals established by the school; and
   - provide transitioning students with mini-classes on a variety of school-related issues such as bell/class schedule, locker navigation, organization techniques and strategies, and social intervention.

- Organize summer orientations such as Jump Start, designed to assist transitioning students and parents with the building orientation and layout.
- Hold a middle school scavenger hunt prior to the beginning of school to assist transitioning students and parents in navigating their new school. This provides an excellent opportunity for incoming students to meet and spend time with teachers and staff.
- Host Early Bird Days, allowing incoming students to start and attend classes two or three days before the rest of the students start school, and Orientation Nights that enable transitioning students to communicate with staff so they can learn about school routines and expectations.

- Arrange school site visits so that students can tour the middle school before they leave the elementary school.
- Assign each elementary student a middle school pen pal and encourage written communication between them.
- Target at-risk students and assign peer or staff mentors the year prior to the transition.

For school leaders:

- Make the planning, implementation, and evaluation of transition activities an annual focus, beginning in the intermediate grades of the elementary school.
- Begin as early as grade five to create an environment that promotes a confident transition from a self-contained classroom structure to the larger team structure of the middle school by enabling students to change classes throughout the day during their last year in elementary school. Many schools do this through team teaching, departmentalization, or advanced scheduling of core classes utilizing an interdisciplinary team of teachers.
- Encourage collaboration among elementary and middle school teachers, students, and parents:
    - Schedule meetings that will bring together students, parents, teachers, and other essential staff members for the purpose of transition planning.
    - Host a Return Day, where students return to their respective elementary schools for the day to discuss their transition to middle school.
    - Permit middle school teachers and counselors to spend a day or two in the elementary schools to meet future students.
    - Host middle school tours to allow students to walk the halls, become familiar with the academic program, review school rules and procedures, meet the staff.

- Provide comprehensive orientation programs for teachers, students, and families, including older siblings, who strongly influence attitudes and perceptions of transitioning students.
- Become knowledgeable about the needs and concerns of young adolescents in transition.
- Support teachers' efforts to address students' social, developmental, and academic needs.
- Provide leadership in creating a climate that values and supports effective home/school communications.

For teachers and counselors:

- Engage in collaborative planning with their counterparts at the elementary and middle levels to ensure a smooth academic transition that recognizes and accommodates variations in curricula across feeder schools.
- Allow the elementary staff and the middle school teachers to trade places for a day so that newly transitioned students can have contact with some of their old teachers, and students preparing for transition can become familiar with their new teachers.
- Become knowledgeable about the needs and concerns of young adolescents in transition.
- Keep parents informed, help them become skilled in dealing with issues related to transition, and welcome their participation in their children's education.
- Provide counseling at both the elementary and middle levels to address transition concerns and assure students of the availability of ongoing support.
- Provide programs, activities, and curricula to help students understand and cope successfully with the challenges of transition.
- Use a variety of developmentally appropriate instructional practices that enable each child to experience academic success.
- Employ strategies such as cooperative learning that provide opportunities for peer interaction.

- Consider organizational structures such as team teaching that ensure teachers have meaningful knowledge and understanding of each child.

For parents:

- Provide young children with manageable tasks that help them develop organizational skills and responsibility.
- Encourage children to try new things and to regard failure as a necessary part of learning and growing.
- Become knowledgeable about the needs and concerns of young adolescents in transition.
- Help children turn their anxieties into positive action by learning about school rules, schedules, locker procedures, and the availability of counseling.
- Attend school functions and stay involved in children's schooling.
- Support children in their efforts to become independent.
- Maintain strong family connections with young adolescents.
- Be alert to signs of depression or anxiety in their children and seek help.

REFERENCES

American Educational Research Association (AERA). (2010). *New strategies for keeping schools safe: Evidence-based approaches to prevent youth violence.* Capitol Hill briefing. Retrieved from http://www.aera.net/Portals/38/docs/About_AERA/KeyPrograms/AERA%20Factsheet-1%20April8-2010.pdf

Dinkes, R., Kemp, J., & Baum, K. (2009). *Indicators of school crime and safety: 2009.* Washington, DC: National Center for Education Statistics, Institute of Education Sciences, US Department of Education, and Bureau of Justice Statistics, Office of Justice Programs, US Department of Justice. (NCES 2010–012/NCJ 228478)

Midgley, C., & Maehr, M.L. (1998). *The Michigan middle school study: Report to participating schools and districts.* Ann Arbor, MI: Combined Program in Education and Psychology, University of Michigan.

National Middle School Association (NMSA). (2006). Success in the middle: A policymaker's guide to achieving quality middle level education. Retrieved from https://www.google.com/url?sa=t&rct=j&q=&esrc=s&source=web&cd=1&ved=0ahUKEwiu8bTz19_YAhVMzFMKHUxJD2EQFggpMAA&url=http%3A%2F%2Fwww.niusileadscape.org%2Fdocs%2FFINAL_PRODUCTS%2FLearningCarousel%2

FNMSA_Policy_Guide.pdf&usg=AOvVaw3fp4szVsPscji_1KwVJ7hE.
National Middle School Association & National Association of Elementary School Principals. (2002). *Supporting students in their transition to middle school: A joint position paper jointly adopted by the National Middle School Association and the National Association of Elementary School Principals.* Retrieved fromhttps://www.google.com/url?sa=t&rct=j&q=&esrc=s&source=web&cd=1&cad=rja&uact=8&ved=0ahUKEwjxuM3e2t_YAhVO7FMKHSS9ArUQFggpMAA&url=http%3A%2F%2Fwww.nppsd.org%2Fimages%2Fshared%2Fvnews%2Fstories%2F525d81ba96ee9%2FTr%2520-%2520Supporting%2520Students%2520in%2520Their%2520Transition%2520to%2520Middle%2520School.pdf&usg=AOvVaw17bJNZfz3EpYSiQBrgE_HT.

3

BECKY'S STORY

Kids are kids, right? They are pretty much the same—or so educators sometimes think. Boys and girls do learn differently. They react to things differently and respond differently to situations they are presented with. Educators must be cautious to revert to a one-size-fits-all mentality. During the transition from elementary school to middle school, teachers and parents need to recognize and respond to the differences between boys and girls to ensure children have seamless and successful transitions to their new school environments.

VIGNETTE

The transition to middle school seemed easy for Tyler. Several years earlier his older brother, Trevor, had also adjusted to middle school routines and expectations with little difficulty. But it was a different story for their younger sister, Becky. The seven-period school day and different teachers for each content area posed a number of challenges for Becky, who was never the most organized child.

A look at Becky's elementary school desk revealed the telltale signs of a budding preadolescent. Papers were not organized; books were heaped to one side. She had to root around for a pencil and paper on which to take notes. But organized or not, all she ever needed in the fifth grade was right there in that desk that she sat at day after day, all year long. Her homework was in there—just give her a few minutes to find it! In fifth grade, she knew what her teacher expected, even if she was not always prepared for the day.

At the middle school, some teachers required homework on a daily basis. Some gave quizzes every week on a designated day, while other teachers surprised students with *pop* quizzes. All of the teachers had targets on the board, and if Becky were prepared enough to write them down in her daily planner, she would have noticed their connection with the daily learning checks and the formative assessment questions.

For the first time in her young scholastic career, Becky began to complain about school. She frequently voiced her frustration about the different teacher expectations from one class to the next, and she complained at having to keep up with the various assignments in each.

As the days went by, Becky grew increasingly upset with school in general, and she began acting out on a regular basis. Her attitude and behavior started to change: Once a happy-go-lucky child, she became a hormonal adolescent on a roller-coaster ride of emotions. It wasn't until Becky's parents received a phone call one afternoon from her principal, Mrs. Smith, that they—teachers and parents—realized they had to do something different.

No one could assume that Becky—just like other incoming sixth graders and her siblings who transitioned before her—would make the transition in the same manner. How quickly educators and parents forget the physiological changes that follow an adolescent into middle school; hormones kick in, braces come on, zits pop out, and some kids develop more—or less—than their grade-level peers. Becky by all means seemed unprepared for the changes, physically, emotionally, academically, and logistically.

RESEARCH

According to Waggoner (1994), many children coming from a self-contained classroom with only one teacher have difficulty adjusting to the multiple transitions or class changes from teacher to teacher and content to content throughout the instructional day in middle school. In elementary schools that structure some degree of class change into their instructional day, students are better prepared for the transition to the middle school than those coming from fully self-contained classroom settings. Sixty-six percent of all students surveyed believed they would be better prepared for seventh grade if they had more than one sixth-grade teacher (in school districts where sixth grade is part of elementary school) (Waggoner, 1994).

A study of 171 sixth graders (Waggoner, 1994) found that students entering middle school from schools that provide team settings that emulate smaller learning communities (SLCs) demonstrate a stronger affiliation in school activities and fewer concerns about the transition than did students in self-contained sixth-grade classrooms. Teachers in team settings felt their students exhibited fewer indicators of stress related to progressing to junior high school than teachers of students in self-contained sixth-grade classrooms.

INTERVENTIONS

How can parents and schools help alleviate the powerful concerns children often have about transitioning to a new school?

The National Middle School Association suggests that parents of transitioning students can alleviate much of the stress commonly associated with the transition to a new school and increase the possibility of successful transition if they are willing to communicate openly and effectively with school officials, teachers, and principals. The list below, organized by the NMSA, suggests interventions by parents that can help with transition (NMSA, 2011).

Schools, especially those that foster self-contained class schedules, can work collaboratively to modify school schedules to allow students some means of a rotation that emulates what they will experience at the middle school.

Schools and parents must work together to address the concerns associated with the transition from one school to the next. Lorain (2011) believes that a planned and intentional, well-structured transition program that involves all stakeholders may just be the key to easing the anxiety associated with transitions. Effective transition plans focus on a holistic approach and are geared toward meeting the social, emotional, and academic needs of the child.

Schumacher (1998) illustrates that effective and comprehensive transition plans include numerous activities geared toward easing of the concerns children have pertaining to their new school environment.

Strategies and Suggestions

The following intervention strategies and suggestions were developed from the research of the National Middle School Association (2011); Lorain (2011); and Gurian, Stevens, Henley, and Trueman (2010).

For schools and teachers:

- Develop comprehensive transition plans that identify the physical, emotional, academic, and social needs of the student. Differentiate instruction to meet individual needs.
- Support communication between teachers of transitioning students and encourage students' new teachers to communicate frequently with their previous teachers.
- Ensure a positive and successful first impression of your school for new students.
- Encourage adequate communication between the school and parents of transitioning students.

- Assign school counselors or other staff members to shadow incoming students to provide any needed support, especially for the first few weeks or months following the transition.
- Structure the elementary and middle school in teams or SLCs where teachers manage a smaller number of students, allowing them to forge personal relationships with each student.
- Become more knowledgeable about the differences between boys and girls and adjust teaching styles and structures to address these differences.

For parents:

- Be alert to signs of depression or anxiety in children and seek help when necessary.
- Encourage children to try new things and to regard failure as a necessary part of learning.
- Become knowledgeable about the needs and concerns of young adolescents.
- Open direct lines of communication with teachers, administrators, and other parents.
- Help children turn their anxieties into positive action by learning about school rules, schedules, locker procedures, and the availability of counseling.
- Attend school functions and stay involved.
- Become good listeners.
- Provide support for children in their efforts to become independent.
- Maintain strong family connections with young adolescents.
- Encourage student participation and involvement in classroom activities and school functions.
- Realize that the more connected a child is to his or her school, the greater the possibility of a successful transition.
- Be proactive whenever possible.

> I like a teacher who gives you something to take home to think about besides homework. —Lily Tomlin as Edith Ann

REFERENCES

Gurian, M., Steven, K., Henley, P., & Trueman, T. (2010). *Boys and girls learn differently: A guide for teachers and parents.* 10 ed. San Francisco, CA: Jossey-Bass.

Lorain, P. (2011). Transition to middle school. Retrieved from http://www.nea.org/tools/16657.htm.

National Middle School Association (NMEA). (2011). Tips for parents. Retrieved from: http://www.nmsa.org/Advocacy/PressRoom/MiddleSchoolEducationNews/Article1/Tips/tabid/394/Default.asp. (Direct link is no longer active.)

Schumacher, D. (1998, June). The Transition to Middle School. Elementary and Early Childhood Education, 1–2.

Waggoner, J.E. (1994, October). *The relationship between instructional teaming and self-esteem of sixth graders transitioning to a traditional junior high.* Paper presented at a meeting of the Illinois Association of Teacher Educators, Lisle, IL. (ED 379 278)

4

TOP DOG EFFECT

Each year hundreds of thousands of school children leave the safe and secure environment of the elementary school into the unknown territory known as middle school. Many of these transitioning students are left to face this period of adjustment—the peer competition, struggles with social acceptance, and physical and emotional changes associated with preadolescence—on their own. It is not uncommon to hear stories of students who excelled in elementary school falling by the wayside upon entering middle school.

High-performing and subsequently high-achieving students are often subjected to the "top dog effect," in which those who have risen to the top in elementary school—by hard work or raw talent—become downtrodden by the negative and sometimes damaging effects of competition following the transition to middle school, where top students from multiple elementary schools vie for athletic, academic, and band positions, to name a few.

It is in middle school that many students experience their first taste of real competition for academic, social, and athletic superiority. For many students, this is their first contact with others as gifted as they are; the star athlete in elementary school, for instance, quickly realizes that he or she is not unique. It is not uncommon to find the former star sitting on the bench during middle school basketball games because the five players were also stars at their elementary schools and are perhaps even more talented.

Competition is a part of life. But how can we as educators better prepare students for the increased competition during this critical transition?

VIGNETTE

Tyler was a good-looking kid who had the loving support of his mother, grandparents, and a host of relatives. Though his mother and father had divorced when he was three years old, he spent considerable time with his father, who still lived in a nearby community. Tyler's story is not one of academic failure or poverty; it is one of social adjustment and the difficulties associated with the transition from a relatively small elementary school into the larger, more impersonal middle school.

During his elementary years, Tyler was *the man* at school. He was a star on his elementary school's basketball team, quarterback on the little league football team, and one of the top academic students in his class. Life was good for Tyler in elementary school, but in middle school, things began crashing down around him.

Like many kids his age, Tyler felt the pressures of social acceptance and a desire to fit in with his new surroundings, and he began to withdraw from many of the things he used to love. He started trying to ditch school by pretending to be sick so that he could spend the day at home in the company of the Xbox and computer.

Tyler's long history of athletic and academic success had hit a bump in the road. His frustrations became apparent at the end of the first month of middle school, when football practice began. It was at this point that be became depressed at his fall from the leader of the team to a second-string player. For the first time, he had real competition for the coveted position of quarterback, one he had always held.

Tyler's attitude and happy-go-lucky demeanor began to change. He began to lose interest in his grades and seldom completed his homework. His frustrations and negative attitude toward his new coach and his new surroundings marked the first time ever that Tyler did not want to play ball. Suddenly, he couldn't care less whether he was on time to practice or even if he played football at all.

It is at this critical juncture in the life of adolescents that educators can have a great impact on their students' lives. When teachers and schools develop transition plans that identify with students' experiences and provide strategies that help students find and develop their talents, they can help ensure transition success for students like Tyler. When transition issues are left unaddressed, it is here that we lose once-promising students to failing grades, increased negative behavior, and a growing feeling of disconnect that often leads to dropping out.

Educators need to be prepared to help students like Tyler find another open door when one seems to be closing. As students advance into higher grade levels, they often find that competition increases. One by one, students who were once engaged fall by the wayside. For others, the door will close later, during the transition into high school, when they are faced with the cold reality that they will not be playing college ball or that their dream of playing in the NBA or NFL has all but disappeared.

During whatever transition a student experiences closed doors, those who are prepared with alternate plans and alternative ways to cope with the reality of closed doors will persevere, exploring and developing their hidden talents and successfully navigating the transition. For students who have no parent to help them cope, educators become their lifeline.

Educators can do better in preparing students to cope with these bumps in the road during their transition. Educators can also work to provide more opportunities for student participation and put processes in place that help teachers build relationships with students; these teachers can then notice when doors are closing for their students and help them find alternative ways to be involved.

RESEARCH

Weiss (1993) suggests that middle school athletic competition can have both positive and negative effects on the preadolescent child. The positive aspects include improvement in the level of physical fitness and self-esteem, while the negative aspects include increased anxiety and stress.

Many of these negative stressors could be eliminated if schools focused on keeping competition in perspective by creating more opportunities that allow children to have fun and enjoy skill development and physical activity beyond competitive sports. The American Academy of Pediatrics (2001) and McEwan and Swaim (2009) suggest that too often the coaches, teachers, or other staff members assigned to supervise athletic events stray from the program's "educational purposes," and that many of these athletic events were not created or designed with the children's best interest in mind.

The Association for Middle Level Education (2012) encourages schools to strongly consider the types of interscholastic sports offered to middle school students, suggesting that schools offer sports focused on individual improvement, such as track and field, swimming, or archery. Studies have found that student participation in these events increases, and should take precedence over competitive sports such as football, basketball, and soccer.

Middle school advisory programs can assist in developing relationships between students and teachers (AMLE, 2012). Teachers who are assigned a small number of students within well-developed advisory programs can monitor student academic, behavioral, and social progress in the transition from elementary school to middle school. These smaller learning communities of teachers and students allow teachers to be on top of things, noticing when a student is no longer an active participant.

School counseling programs cannot possibly serve the needs of all students in a school. Advisory programs can serve as a process for keeping a watchful eye on each and every student, so that all students are more connected to the whole school program and have a mentor or coach to lend support and advice along the way.

INTERVENTIONS

For many students, interventions need to begin as early as the fourth grade (AMLE, 2012). Elementary schools should strive to provide interactions designed to introduce friendly competition with students from other schools in the same district. This could be done by conducting academic team competitions, spelling bees, or a variety of athletic competitions and intramural programs. In many districts, children can be placed on combined teams to compete with other districts.

Most of us are familiar with a variety of all-star teams that bring together the combined talents of many children in a variety of sports. All-star teams can have a positive impact on transitioning students because they allow particularly talented students to develop relationships with one another before they are pitted against one another in competition for the same positions upon entering the middle school.

Strategies and Suggestions

The following intervention strategies and suggestions for schools and teachers were developed from the research of the Association for Middle Level Education (2012) and Weiss (1993).

- Ensure that the educational focus of all athletic competition is designed to meet adolescent children's needs by laying the groundwork for a healthy lifestyle involving physical activity by
    - increasing the physical fitness level of the child;
    - developing the fine motor skills; and

- developing of leadership skills, socialization skills, and self-esteem.
- Ensure that all extracurricular activities focus less on competition and more on skill development, and allow all interested students to participate.
- Provide all coaches and assistants with adequate training such as coaching certification training, safety and first aid training, and competency-based training that includes rules clinics for all activities being supervised.
- Ensure that all activities and sports provide each participant the opportunity to develop skills, improve self-esteem, gain leadership experience, and become a member of a team.
- Focus on team-building skills.

REFERENCES

American Academy of Pedatrics: Committee on Sports Medicine and Fitness and Committee on School Health. (2001). Organized sports for children and preadolescents. *Pediatrics* 107.6 (2001). Retrieved from http://pediatrics.aappublications.org/content/107/6/1459.

Association for Middle Level Education (AMLE). (2012). Co-curricular physical activity and programs for middle school students: A position statement by the national association for sport and physical education's (NASPE) middle and secondary school physical education council. http://www.amle.org/AboutAMLE/PositionStatements/SportPrograms/tabid/292/Default.aspx .

McEwan, C. K., and Swaim, J. (2009). Research Summary: Middle level interscholastic sports programs. Retrieved from http://www.amle.org/TabId/270ArtMID/888/ArticleID/324/Research-Summary-Middle-Level-INterscholastic-Sports-Programs.aspx.

Weiss, M. (1993). Self-esteem and achievement in children's sport and physical activity. In D. Gould & M. R. Weiss (Eds.), *Advances in pediatric sport sciences* (pp. 87–119). Champaign, IL: Human Kinetics.

5

AFRAID TO TAKE A CHANCE

Not all students negatively impacted in the transition from elementary school to middle school come from rural, low-income homes.

Struggles during the transition from elementary school to middle school are common to kids from all walks of life: rural, inner city, and suburban, poor and affluent alike. The stories of middle- and upper-class kids differ somewhat from those of others. These children may have nice homes, warm clothing to wear, plenty of food to eat, and possibly even two parents residing in their home, but they struggle nonetheless. Many of these kids are suffocating under the weight of the expectations of their parents and pressure from their peers to not appear either too smart or too dumb.

Regardless of demographics, children from middle- and upper-class households have similar experiences, concerns, and needs as their peers from lower-income homes. These preadolescent and adolescent children feel anger, despair, and a sense of losing control of themselves. Combined with the onset of puberty, fear of rejection, and the uncertainty involved with the transition to middle school, many of these students begin to develop a fixed mind-set and shy away from challenging learning opportunities at which they could potentially excel.

A fixed mind-set causes students to take the easy route to success, fearing the possibility of failure in more challenging opportunities. *Often students will begin to refrain from asking questions in class or participating in class discussions for fear of saying something wrong or looking dumb in front of their peers. Even worse, at this age students often begin to fear looking smart—when smart is not always cool.*

VIGNETTE

Kathy was a twelve-year-old from a good home. Her dad was an engineer and her mom was an account manager at a local bank. She was the middle child in a loving and supportive household. Her younger brother, age seven, attended the suburban elementary school she had just left. Her older sister was seventeen, a junior in high school and contender for class valedictorian faced with the agonizing task of deciding which Ivy League school she would attend upon graduation.

Kathy had always been a very bright and pleasant child. As an elementary student she loved school and could not wait to see her peers every morning. But during the first weeks after her transition to middle school, Kathy's teachers began to notice a change in her behavior. She no longer wished to participate in classroom discussions and seldom ever raised her hand to ask questions or provide input during classroom activities. A few of her teachers attempted to praise her intelligence and encouraged her to become more involved in class discussions, but even though her teachers made numerous attempts to engage her more fully, she withdrew at every opportunity.

This once bright and often outspoken student had now retreated into a world of silence. When asked why she had suddenly become so shy, she explained, "I do not want to look stupid and yet . . . I do not want to look smart either." Kathy had become obsessed with the fear that her friends would laugh at her if she was wrong—or if she appeared too intellectual.

At this time in her growth and development, it was more important to Kathy that she fit in with her peers, and she didn't want to be perceived as smart or stupid, either of which could make her an outcast. Combined with this, the pressure at home to live up to her older sister's ambition and intellectual gifts further complicated life in middle school for Kathy. Her parents had even greater expectations for Kathy than they'd had for her sister, and during the first few weeks of middle school, her teachers all commented, "If you are anything like your sister, we have great expectations for you!"

Incoming students at the middle school had the opportunity to enroll in experimental, elite honors English class, but Kathy chose not to take this class. She did not want to risk being labeled *smart*— or risk getting a grade lower than an A. So she played it safe, preferring to blend in rather than being out front and on top like her sister.

Kathy always saw her sister leading the class while receiving all kinds of awards and accolades. But she also noticed that her sister never went on dates, did not belong to the "in crowd," and never went to prom. She saw her sister concentrating so much on grades that it seemed she never had time for doing what kids do. Kathy did not want to emulate this same behavior. Kathy wanted her own identity. She wanted to find her own way. She wanted to develop her own gifts and not become what her sister was.

During the first parent-teacher conference, Kathy's homeroom teacher, Mrs. Salyers, discussed with Kathy's parents her growing concerns. The teacher explained that several of Kathy's other teachers assigned participation grades in their classes, and as a result a couple grades in Kathy's core classes were low due to her lack of participation.

Both of her parents were dismayed by what they were hearing. They reacted by grounding Kathy until they saw marked improvement in her grades and participation. Kathy's parents had always set high expectations for their children, and it was difficult for them to accept that she might receive anything less than an A in every subject. They immediately signed Kathy up for the honors class.

RESEARCH

Dweck (2010), a noted author and psychologist, has spent three decades studying the factors at play in student motivation. Most of her research centers on the question of why some students display resilience, persistence, and enjoyment of learning, even though the subject matter may pose a degree of difficulty, while others tend to shut down, turn off, and shy away from intellectual material they find challenging. Dweck suggests that students have either a fixed or a growth mind-set, and that their ability to be successful in challenging learning experiences depends upon the mind-set of the individual.

Students who have a fixed mind-set are more inclined to shy away from pursuits that tend to be challenging, difficult, or pose the possibility of failure, thus limiting their ability to take risks. Students who possess a growth mind-set often seek out and gravitate toward academic pursuits that offer the greatest degree of difficulty—and often the greatest potential for learning—and are more likely to take calculated risks pertaining to learning experiences (Dweck, 2010).

Students with a fixed mind-set often have greater difficulty with transitions and dealing with failure (Dweck, 2010). These students are less willing to take risks and shy away from more challenging classes for fear of earning a lower grade. Add this to the complexities of adolescence and it is easy to see why so many first-year middle school students have such difficulty with the transition to the middle school.

Dweck (2010) posits that mind-set is developed largely as a result of the type of classroom assignments students are given and the kind of praise they receive from their teachers, parents, and peers. She asserts that the wrong kind of praise can actually be damaging to students, cautioning educators to never praise a student's intelligence but instead to should praise a student's work ethic or willingness to stick with a task when the going gets tough.

According to Dweck (2008), "[E]ducators commonly hold two beliefs that are false or even harmful." The first of these is that praising students' intelligence builds motivation to learn and the second is that students' inherent intelligence is the major cause of their achievement in school. Dweck writes, "Our research has shown the first belief to be false, and the second can be harmful—even for the most competent students because praise is intricately connected to how students view their intelligence" (p. 34).

Dweck believes that students who are praised for their intelligence develop a fixed mind-set and become excessively concerned with how smart they are, seeking tasks that will prove their intelligence and avoiding those that don't. Students who possesses this mind-set often shy away from any learning opportunity at which they might make a mistake or be perceived as a failure. As a result, learning takes a backseat (Dweck, 2006). In short, "praising students' intelligence gives them a short burst of pride, followed by a long string of negative consequences" (Mueller & Dweck 1998, p. 33).

Students with growth mind-sets tend to be less concerned with how smart they might appear to others and are better prepared to bounce back after life's little setbacks. Dweck (2006) claims that her research, which has followed students through challenging school transitions and tough classes, found that students with growth mind-sets outperform their classmates with fixed mind-sets even when they entered school with equal skills and knowledge.

Schools would benefit from offering transition activities that encourage students to take risks and provide support systems for those risk takers.

INTERVENTIONS

Assisting the preadolescent child in developing a positive self-image, age-appropriate academic skills, a growth mind-set, and an overall interest in learning should be a priority for all schools. Learning how to achieve this for middle school students sometimes poses a challenge. Mullins and Irvin (2000) suggest that the physical, social, and emotional changes often triggered by puberty, added to the stresses of transitioning to a new school environment, present tremendous obstacles for many preadolescent students.

Strategies and Suggestions

The following intervention strategies and suggestions for schools, teachers, and parents were developed from the research of Maxwell (2000) and Dweck (2006, 2008).

- Establish early on that failing is part of growing and learning. Teachers should ensure that students are presented with challenging instructional practices geared toward their instructional level.
- Parents, teachers, and school counselors should communicate with preadolescent children to ensure that they understand that failure is part of progress. Explain that it is not imperative that they know all the answers all the time and that learning is often the result of failed attempts to get something right.
- Ensure that children understand the difference between positive and negative risk taking.
- Teachers and parents should refrain from feedback that focuses on children's perceived intelligence because it causes them to withdraw from tasks that may present a degree of challenge, preventing learning experiences from occurring.
- Consider consultation with a counselor at the onset of a student's withdrawal from class discussion and answering direct questions, or at the first sign of fear or anxiety pertaining to participation in class.
- Parents should be in constant communication with teachers and guidance counselors pertaining to their children's progress in school, especially during the transition year.
- Praise students' attempts to answer questions, participation in class, and hard work and effort put into assignments.
- Help students discover and develop a growth mind-set.

- Provide support structures and encourage students to be willing to give 100 percent every day.
- Discuss the positive outcomes of taking calculated or positive risks and embrace students' willingness to do so.

REFERENCES

Dweck, C.S. (2006). *Mindset: The new psychology of success*. New York, NY: Random House.
Dweck, C.S. (2008). The perils of promises and praise. *The Best of Educational Leadership 2007–2008, 65*, 34–39.
Dweck, C.S. (2010). Even geniuses work hard. *Educational Leadership, 68*, 16–20.
Maxwell, J.C. (2000). *Failing forward: Turning mistakes into stepping stones for success*. Nashville, TN: Thomas Nelson.
Mueller, C.M. & Dweck, C.S. (1998). Intelligence praise can undermine motivation and performance. *Journal of Personality and Social Psychology, 75*, 33–52.
Mullins, E.R. & Irvin, J.L. (2000). Transition into middle school: What research says. *Middle School Journal, 31*(3), 57–60.

6

SELF-ACTUALIZATION

This story is about the effects transition to middle school had on a teacher's kid. Surprisingly, many of these children experience the same issues pertaining to transitions that other children from different households experience. For most children whose parents are teachers, the pressure to excel in academics is greatly increased.

For parents who are educators who have had very little experience or opportunity to work with students at the middle school level, lack of understanding of the physiological, social, and cognitive changes these children are going through only compounds the problem. As most middle school teachers will confess, middle school is truly a different world. The lessons learned in a far removed Human Growth and Development class taken years earlier when the parent was a college student preparing for a career in the educational field may seem vaguely familiar.

VIGNETTE

Johnny was often hazed by some of his peers because he was a teacher's child. Other students taunted him, claiming he received special privileges as a result. This made Johnny, who had previously been a studious boy, hesitant to apply himself. Already being teased for getting so-called special privileges, he worried that being viewed as a straight-A student would only add to the problem. Like many other middle school children, he only wanted to fit in with the crowd, even if that meant not being studious. He didn't want to be labeled a *nerd*.

Under the stress of trying to be popular, he began to fall behind on his schoolwork, ultimately falling further behind with each passing assignment. When the first grading period ended, Johnny's parents weren't pleased. His father—a teacher who had set high expectations for him—was severely disappointed. After attending the parent-teacher conference held at his school and upon reviewing his son's report card, Johnny's father began to blame the students he hung out with as the reason Johnny was doing so poorly. His father was determined to have some of Johnny's classes changed, and he was grounded him from many of the after-school events he liked to attend. As a result, Johnny began to resent school even more.

As the year progressed, Johnny's difficulties in school seemed to heighten. As he struggled to find himself and connect with his peers, he began to resent that his father was a teacher. On one occasion his rebellious behavior nearly resulted in in-school suspension for lashing out at his pre-algebra teacher, Mr. Stiggins, who had questioned him about his unfinished homework and threatened to contact his father. This infuriated Johnny, and his verbal reaction to the teacher landed him in the principal's office for the first time since he had started school.

The principal, Mr. Jackson, sat Johnny down and asked him why he had misbehaved. "I don't like this place" was his only reply. After a serious talk with Mr. Jackson, Johnny began to understand why he was in this predicament. He confessed that he didn't appreciate the other kids teasing him because of his father's position, and that he was purposely rebelling because of it. Instead of punishing him, Mr. Jackson was determined to help Johnny navigate this situation.

Mr. Jackson asked Johnny whether, when he was older, he would rather be successful and viewed as a man who'd accomplished his goals in life, or seen as an unsuccessful man who'd accomplished nothing. As Mr. Jackson began mentoring to Johnny, the boy's worry and apprehension began to subside.

During this process, Mr. Jackson's mentoring turned into a means of intervention, and Johnny began to develop a connection with his principal. Luckily for Johnny, Mr. Jackson had three sons of his own and could relate to Johnny's struggle. Mr. Jackson shared with him a similar situation one of his sons had experienced when he was about Johnny's age.

As a result of his mentoring sessions with Mr. Jackson, Johnny began to question his own motives for success. Had the overrated status of being one of the "cool kids" become more important to him than doing well in school? As a result of this mentorship with his principal, Johnny to reevaluated his scholastic goals and began to realize his true potential and the importance of his education.

RESEARCH

The research indicates that having positive adult mentors typically results in successful developmental outcomes for adolescent children. Mentoring relationships often serve to positively impact adolescents' self-perceptions, attitudes, and behaviors (Walker & Freedman 1996). Evidence also suggests that, for many troubled adolescents, the mentor/mentee relationship is thought to indirectly improve communications between parent and child by providing support with communication skills, conflict mediation, and age-appropriate coping skills (Rhodes, Haight, & Briggs, 1999).

Further research conducted by Big Brothers Big Sisters of America (BBBSA) suggests that community- and school-based mentoring programs reduce many barriers for school-aged children. Keoki Hansen, director of research and evaluation for BBBSA, suggests that mentoring programs such as these can effectively increase academic performance, create and support an improved attitude toward school, improve peer and parental relationships, helping to ensure high school graduation (Hansen, 2007).

Many schools across the country find success in easing the fears and anxiety for incoming middle school students through the use of peer mentors as a transition activity. Peer mentors are most often chosen from among the upperclassmen (typically eighth graders), and each is assigned an incoming sixth grader to mentor throughout the transitional year. Child psychologists agree that most transitioning students have difficulty with many of the changes experienced by preadolescent and adolescent children as they transition from elementary to middle school—including meeting new friends, dealing with peer pressure, and increasingly depending on peers for self-concept and personal identity—in addition to navigating the changes in environment, teachers, assignments/homework, and in educational practices of the new school.

These anxieties can be significantly reduced by peer mentoring, according to research published by the Mentoring Resource Center (2008), which found that "cross-age peer mentoring programs take advantage of adolescents' increasing interest in peer friendships as they enter the teenage years, often building new relationships beyond their normal circle of friends" (p. 7).

Another notable point in support of implementing peer mentoring programs during the transition is that such programs select students from within their own schools. Because of this, the costs often associated with recruitment and retention of adult mentors are eliminated, making peer mentoring programs not only productive but cost effective as well. (Mentoring Resource Center, 2008).

INTERVENTIONS

Research has established the importance of the powerful impact a mentor can have on the adolescent student. Mentors serve to provide a personal and nonjudgmental connection to their mentees that parents and peer groups often do not. The suggestions in the list that follows offer food for thought for schools considering developing mentor programs to assist with transitions.

Strategies and Suggestions:

The following intervention strategies and suggestions for schools and teachers were developed from the research of Big Brothers and Big Sisters of America (Hansen, 2007); the Mentoring Resource Center (2008); Walker and Freedman (1996); and Rhodes, Haight, and Briggs (1999).

- Understand the importance of positive adult role models and adult mentor programs and seek to establish those connections within the schools.
- Develop comprehensive transition and mentoring programs that assist students in adapting to their new environment, establish reachable and realistic goals, and clarify expectations.
- Plan for and include transition activities in school and district improvement plans.
- Establish a Middle School Prep Camp, a two-day event held in the summer prior to opening of school. Goals of this program include

    - aiding in reducing students' stress;
    - allowing students to begin making new friends; and
    - reducing anxiety commonly associated with opening day.

- Utilize peer mentoring programs in which each incoming student is assigned an upperclassman to serve as a mentor for the transition year. Training and supervision of peer mentors is paramount and should start prior to opening day. During an introductory meeting over the summer with mentors, incoming students, and parents:

    - allow mentors to take the incoming students on a tour of the building;
    - incorporate time for dialogue to ensure student success; and

- have "Locker Relays" to allow students to practice navigating the lockers and unlocking the combination locks.

REFERENCES

Hansen, K. 2007. *One-to-one mentoring: Literature review*. Philadelphia, PA: Big Brothers and Big Sisters of America.

Mentoring Resource Center (2008). *Building effective peer mentoring programs in schools: An introductory guide*. Folsom, CA: Author.

Rhodes, J.E., Haight, W.L., & Briggs, E.C. (1999). The influence of mentoring on the peer relationships of foster youth in relative and non-relative care. *Journal of Research on Adolescence, 2,* 185–202.

Walker, G. & Freedman, M. (1996). Social change one on one: The new mentoring movement. *American Prospect, 27,* 75–81.

7

SO EACH MAY LEARN

The data, research, and vignettes in this book present substantiating evidence that the social and emotional impact associated with transitions for preadolescent children are immense. Even the best and brightest students often experience difficulties as they are propelled into the uncertain world of transition. Even for the most well-adjusted students, preadolescence, combined with the onset of puberty and an internal drive to seek independence, can pose challenges.

Most children have positive support structures in place to assist them with this difficult time in their young lives; others do not. Imagine then the impact of transition for a special needs child, more specifically, a child diagnosed with an autism spectrum disorder or Asperger syndrome. Educators have only recently begun to understand the social, emotional, and physiological needs of children with autism.

In the past decade, schools across the country have started to focus on these needs, with workshops and trainings offered more frequently, perhaps due in part to the rising number of identified cases. With a better understanding of autism, teachers are becoming better prepared to meet the needs of these children and better equipped to assist in acclimating these students to the world in which they live and the new school environments to which they are transitioning.

VIGNETTE

Susan was an amazing eleven-year-old who had recently been diagnosed with autism spectrum disorder, also referred to as pervasive developmental disorder. She was described as a "high-functioning special needs student," with below average social skills as compared to her peer group. She was somewhat aloof and often much slower to engage in social interactions. Her interests included music, animals (particularly horses), and watching movies and popular TV sitcoms. Susan frequently quoted lines from movies and sitcoms she had seen. Although this reaction sometimes seemed to others as being out of context, the quotes usually had a direct connection to the events surrounding her.

Susan also exhibited frequent repetitive movements such as rocking back and forth and excessive wringing and shaking of her hands and fingers, as if trying to shake water from them. She often had muffled conversations with herself and was highly excitable and anxious, especially during assemblies, lunch, and recess, as a result of the loud noise and movement of other children during these events. She often took literally the comments or statements of others and she became easily upset when other children were arguing or engaged in heated debate.

Susan's elementary principal, Mrs. Williams, described her as being fairly successful in elementary school. She read at a fourth-grade level, interacted positively with her peers, and loved watching movies, frequently reciting tag lines and dialogue from movies she had seen. Mrs. Williams categorized Susan's overall experience in her school as a delightful and enjoyable one. Mrs. Williams stated that Susan had many friends around her who were always anxious to assist her, noting specifically that these children had gone to school with Susan since kindergarten and were very receptive of her needs.

Mrs. Williams pointed out that in many respects, Susan was much like her peers, indicating that her staff had received numerous hours of training in order to better meet her academic and physiological needs. Mrs. Williams felt strongly that the professional development in which she and her staff participated "opened the door to possibilities" for Susan and other special needs children like her.

Mrs. Williams shared an anecdote of a minor discipline issue during the time Susan was at her school. Overhearing an inappropriate comment Susan made to a male peer, the teacher wasn't sure how to handle it and asked the principal to speak with the child. Susan's comment allegedly was a quote from a popular movie, and though she perhaps never intended it to be communicated audibly, it had landed her in the principal's office.

Per protocol, the principal began the discussion with Susan by explaining what were acceptable behaviors at school with regard to comments made by students to one another. She continued by reminding Susan of the discipline code of acceptable behavior, pointing out that such actions could warrant detention or even suspension from school.

Susan then asked what *suspension* was, and Mrs. Williams gave her a related example: If a teacher does or says something unacceptable he or she could be sent home or fired. The child then asked, "So are you going to fire me?" Before the principal could say anything further, Susan crossed her arms, leaned back in her chair, and piped out, "Well, you can't fire me, because I quit!"

When Susan entered middle school at the beginning of sixth grade, she found herself not only in a new school setting but in a different world altogether. The middle school staff worked collaboratively with Susan's elementary teachers to develop transition activities for her, making numerous phone calls and site visits to the elementary school she had attended, and communicating with her parents, teachers, and former principal.

These actions were duly noted in her Individualized Education Program (IEP) transition plan as a part of the transition requirements pertaining to special education students in her school district. Even though many attempts were made to aid Susan in this transition, she nonetheless had numerous adjustment issues in adapting to her new surroundings and routines.

For Susan, this transition meant she was no longer surrounded by the peer group she had known since beginning school. In fact, she had very little contact with many of her former classmates as a result of the middle school's schedule and the vast population of students also transitioning to the middle school from the district's five elementary schools.

Though she was under the watchful eye of the special education teacher and the aide assigned to assist her, adjustment was slow for Susan. Many of her new classmates were not as accepting of her and were less tolerant of her sensory issues and behaviors. Obviously, this only added to the complexity of her transition to middle school. At one point her parents even considered other educational options for their child.

As the year progressed, so did Susan's adjustment to middle school life. Slowly she began to develop new friendships and daily routines. Her teachers assisted her with transition activities that fostered social interaction with other peers. Counselors developed transition activities that provided information to teachers about how to handle and respond appropriately to autism spectrum disorders and the importance of creating routines and rituals.

Though there were most certainly bumps along the way, in time Susan managed to acclimate to her new environment. She joined the band and developed a passion for art. Her successful transition to middle school was the result of collaborative efforts of the school staff, the resources available, and the planned interventions and modifications aimed at helping guide her as she adjusted, enabling her to stay in public school with her peers.

RESEARCH

It is estimated that well over a million people in the United States suffer from autism or autism spectrum disorders (ASD), also commonly referred to as pervasive developmental disorders (PDD), making autism and its subgroups one of the largest and fastest-growing developmental disorders in our country (Simpson et al., 2005). The Centers for Disease Control and Prevention (CDC) indicate that ASD affects one in every eighty-eight children, and boys are five times more likely to be affected than girls (CDC, 2010).

Early diagnosis of ASD is essential to reduce the negative impact of this disorder and to ensure the child receives the needed interventions. Willis (2009) articulates the importance of "early intervention offering behavioral, social, and skill-building training" for children diagnosed with ASD, noting that "most children with ASD need an Individual Family Service Plan (IFSP) or Individual Education Plan (IEP) in place by the time they enter the classroom," as this is critical to their prognosis.

These plans often differ significantly with regard to to treatment and care because they are designed for the individual child and symptoms. Willis (2009) suggests that educators and family members of children with ASD should "view the child as a person with talents, strengths, and potential" reminding us that educators should focus on what the child can learn as opposed to what he or she cannot.

The research by Simpson and coauthors implies that there is no silver bullet intervention for children with ASD; they recommend instead that caregivers utilize a variety of best practice methods in delivery of interventions. As noted earlier, our knowledge and understanding of autism and ASD has grown dramatically over the past two decades, as more children than ever before are being diagnosed with this developmental disorder.

The strategies provided by specific research on students with ASD are still indistinguishable from those for students without ASD on how to decrease the impact associated with transitioning from one level of schooling to the next. The research does, however, advocate focusing on developing routines and strategies that serve to treat the individual symptoms of each child rather than the transition itself.

INTERVENTIONS

Effective interventions for most special needs children are a critical component of the successful transition between schools. For children like Susan, with autism or autism spectrum disorders, these interventions are often a lifeline, assisting them in adapting to a new school environment. Staff development training and professional development are a must if educators are to stay abreast of the new treatments and interventions for children with autism and its subcategories.

Strategies and Suggestions

The following intervention strategies and suggestions for schools and teachers were developed from the research of the Autism Society of America (2006), Stitcher and Conroy (2006), and Willis (2009).

For teachers:

- Role modeling
- Peer mediation instruction
- Video self-modeling involves short video segments modeling correct procedures to provide students with visual support. This is ideal for common areas with established routines, such as the cafeteria, hallway, and playground.
- Picture Exchange Communication System (PECS) provides students with illustrative example using pictures of procedures and activities to be targeted, serving as a quick visual reference.
- Discrete trail teaching provides gentle on-the-spot correction of improper behavior.
- Use picture labels along with written words on classroom items such as desks, tables, computers, etc.
- Children with autism or ASD typically experience symptomatic anxiety and difficulty transitioning between activities. Plan for and develop smooth transitions from one activity to another:

- Use music to notify the child when switching from one event to another.
- Use a timer or hourglass to signify when it is time to change activities.
- Utilize proximity or a gentle tap on the shoulder to signify to the child that it is time to transition to another class or activity.

• Provide age appropriate social skills training for children with ASD to help them develop social skills that support positive peer interaction. These interventions should begin as early as possible and continue throughout the child's education.
• Create learning centers in various locations throughout the classroom. Centers should include cooperative learning situations as well as "pair share" and small group activities to support positive social interactions with other group members.

For parents:

- Early diagnosis and treatment is critical. If you notice developmental symptoms, seek medical evaluation immediately.
- Assist in the development of the IEP and IFSP.
- Seek membership in organizations focused on current research practices such as the Autism Society of America, the National Association for the Education of Young Children, and regional organizations such as the Autism Society of the Bluegrass. Networking and researching are critical.
- Stay abreast of new research and interventions for children with autism or ASD.
- Ensure two-way communications between parents, teachers, and doctors of children with ASD.

REFERENCES

Autism Society of America. (2006). Autism facts. Retrieved from http://www.autism-society.org. (Direct link is no longer active.)

Centers for Disease Control and Prevention. (2010). New data on autism spectrum disorders. Retrieved from http://www.cdc.gov/ncbddd/autism/delta.html.

Simpson, R.L., de Boer-Ott, S.R., Grisworld, D.E., Myles, B.S., Byrd, S.E., Ganz, J.B., Cook, K.T., Otten, K.L., Ben-Arieh, J., Kline, S.A., & Adams, L.G. (2005). *Autism spectrum disorders: Interventions and treatments for children and youth.* Thousand Oaks, CA: Corwin Press.

Stichter, J.P., & Conroy, M.A. (2006). *How to teach social skills and plan for peer social interactions.* Series on autism spectrum disorders. Austin, TX: Pro-Ed.

Willis, C. (2009). Young children with autism spectrum disorder: Strategies that work. *Beyond the Journal, 63,* 1–8. Retrieved from http://www.naeyc.org/yc/pastissues/2009/january. (Link is no longer active.)

8

SIGHT UNSEEN

Parents and educators have a common goal: to see children grow to become self-sufficient, knowledgeable, independent adults. Navigation of this course begins at birth and directly involves the public school as children enter preschool or kindergarten and culminates as they graduate high school. Effective transition plans for students as they advance through the schools are critically important to their success.

Most students and adults possess the ability to physically see the world as they try to navigate their way through it; many have the gift of sight yet never fully come to appreciate that gift and what it has to offer. For visually impaired students, navigating transitions can be even more difficult, requiring more comprehensive transition plans. Transition plans for special needs children transcend the routine school-to-school transitions often associated with movement from one school to the next, such as the transition from elementary to middle school.

The implementation of federal mandates, the Individualized Education Program, and transition planning services levels the playing field for many students with disabilities. Once students reach sixteen years of age, transition services begin to take on a new role beyond improving classroom instruction to meet their needs; they also pro-

vide students with authentic, real-world learning experiences within the community.

The American Foundation for the Blind (n.d.) describes these services as a "coordinated set of activities based on students' needs, taking into account individual preferences and interests." The transition plan is designed to be a results-oriented process, focused on improving the academic and functional achievement of students with disabilities, and facilitating students' movement from school to posteducational activities.

VIGNETTE

Luke was a talented young man who possessed a sharp mind and keen sense of awareness. He was born with a rare form of optic atrophy that causes blindness. Because of this, he never had the opportunities that many of his peers often take for granted, such as watching the sun rise and set, seeing the faces of his mom and dad, or sitting in the classroom staring at the walls plastered with visual aids.

Luke suffered from genetic glaucoma and could not see the world as other kids do. Because of his visual impairment, Luke developed his other senses to the point that he "saw" things by the way they smell, sound, or feel. In many respects, Luke saw life more clearly than many others who possessed the gift of sight all their life.

When Luke started primary school, he was assigned an instructional assistant to help him adjust to his new school environment. His assistant frequently consulted with his teachers and transferred his work into Braille. Though Luke was fortunate to have two very supportive parents, neither of them could entertain the thought of sending him off to the state school for the blind, which was 150 miles from home. They were determined that he could learn and achieve alongside his peers. They provided a loving and nurturing home for Luke and advocated on his behalf to ensure that he received a quality education in the public school setting.

Both parents attended all scheduled school meetings and played an active role in designing Luke's IEP. His parents expected that Luke would grow and mature into an independent man, graduate college, and someday hold a job. They encouraged him to use a cane for mobility, both at home and at school. They encouraged him to help himself and not rely solely on the assistance of others to guide him around. Luke's self-esteem was always very high. He never wanted pity from others, nor did he expect it.

Academically, Luke was a very bright student. He had well above average math skills and could read Braille faster than many of his peers could read printed text. Cognitively, Luke experienced very little difficulty learning other than that posed by his visual impairment. He was always eager to learn new things, and he loved to be challenged.

Transitioning Luke from elementary school to middle school, however, posed some challenges, requiring more strategic planning from his teachers. This move proved to be one of Luke's most challenging transitions, but his positive attitude and willingness to navigate whatever obstacles life put in his way enabled him to persevere.

Luke came from a small elementary school environment with a family atmosphere that was nurturing and very supportive. In each year of elementary school, Luke had only one teacher who taught all disciplines, requiring very little movement from one class to the next, with the exception of art and physical education. The small size of his class also enabled him to become very secure within this setting. When he moved into the middle school environment, he found it somewhat less nurturing and more focused on independence. In addition, he had a more demanding and rigorous schedule, with seven different teachers each day.

Fortunately, Luke had a strong transition plan in place that included several site visits to the middle school during his last year in the elementary grades. These visits enabled Luke to become familiar with the building layout and travel routines. Braille room numbers were posted throughout the building, and he was introduced to the people who would be his new teachers during each transition activity visit.

Just prior to Luke's arrival at the middle school, the staff received training and professional development to ensure they were prepared to meet the challenges Luke was likely to face as he transitioned into their school. Each of his teachers reviewed his IEP and provided input for the implementation of his individual transition plan. This training made them mindful of how to plan for instruction, how to provide feedback specifically to Luke, and how to effectively ask him questions in class. Teachers learned how to integrate more auditory learning into each lesson, how to effectively deliver tactile learning experiences in classroom instruction, and to be careful about asking questions such as "What do you see?" or "What does this look like?"—which required sight to answer.

The middle school teachers were a bit apprehensive about receiving Luke and concerned about their ability to meet his learning needs, but as school began and the days turned to weeks, Luke transitioned smoothly to the new middle school environment. His teachers realized their fears were unfounded as they collaborated to find solutions to any obstacles they faced in helping him. Luke's ability to effectively transition to middle school was primarily the result of the efforts of his teachers, administrators, and parents, who spent many hours planning, training, and developing his transition plan in advance.

RESEARCH

The terms *blind* and *visually impaired* are often used synonymously. It is important, however, to acknowledge that all individuals who are blind are visually impaired, but not all visually impaired students are blind (American Foundation for the Blind).

For parents and educators of visually impaired children, the old adage "seeing is believing" should be replaced with "achieving is believing." An article from the website of the National Federation of the Blind argues just that, noting that "the value parents place on their child's independent movement and travel has a great deal to do with how he or she will move in the world" (Cutter, 1997, p. 1).

Parents and teachers who support and even encourage the independent mobility of blind children greatly impact the development of their self-esteem and sense of autonomy (Cutter, 1997). If the goal for blind children is to mature and grow into competent, self-sufficient, independent adults, they must be encouraged to navigate their own paths.

According to Cutter (1997), proper support and training is essential for students and teachers working with students with disabilities. Too many visually impaired children do not succeed in achieving independence. The majority of these students never hold legitimate employment and remain dependent upon parents or others for support the remainder of their lives. This cycle of dependence could be broken if schools develop transition plans designed to promote and teach independence.

According to Cameto & Nagle (2007), in the United States only about 28 percent of visually impaired individuals who have completed high school are employed. If our goal is to ensure that these young people are able to become productive and independent members of society, specific attention must be given to address their transitional needs into the posteducational phase of life.

Under current federal guidelines, visually impaired students have transition plans built into their IEPs. Not only does this transition planning process assist the visually impaired students with effective school to school transitions, but it also focuses more on long-term goals, ensuring that these students are prepared for life after school. The IEP planning process brings together community service providers, family members, and the student to create a roadmap for success by providing information about postsecondary training options and community resources available (American Foundation for the Blind, n.d.).

Individuals who are made to feel, different, incompetent, or inadequate often suffer from low self-esteem. For many visually impaired children, these feelings will negatively impact how they fit in the world around them, and this negative impact often directly correlates to their educational achievement (Bowen, 2010).

When comparing an individual's self-perception and academic achievement level, it becomes apparent that if the two are in sync, the student's self-esteem will remain high. Visually impaired children who possess high self-esteem will often push themselves to excel in academic pursuits and obtain a higher level of independence (Cameto & Nagle, 2007).

INTERVENTIONS

A common goal of organizations such as the American Foundation for the Blind and the National Federation of the Blind is to educate and inform others of the natural abilities and talents that blind and visually impaired people possess. Those who work with visually impaired students quickly realize their instinctive abilities and personal drive to be both mobile and included in daily routines.

Strategies and Suggestions

The following tips for teachers and caregivers of visually impaired students as key transition activities from elementary school to middle school are adapted from Castellano (1991).

- Establish a goal of independence:

    - Realize that visually impaired children need the same information, education, and life experiences that others do.
    - Realize that visually impaired children use alternative techniques other than eyesight to achieve these goals.

- Develop the skill sets of the visually impaired child:

    - Utilize and teach Braille reading and writing.

- Encourage and teach use of a cane for mobility.
- Incorporate tactile learning experiences during instruction.
- Utilize auditory aids and encourage students to examine physical objects by touch rather than sight.
- Develop memory skills.
- Develop sound localization skills.
- Teach visually impaired students to ask questions such as "Who is speaking?" or "Who is walking down the hallway?"

- Communicate effectively:

  - Use clear, specific directions such as "fold the paper lengthwise" instead of "fold the paper in half."
  - Explain illustrations in the reading material.
  - Clearly discuss and explain expected routines.

- Provide assistance, but do not do it for them:

  - Encourage support staff (aides and volunteers) to assist but to not do things for them.
  - Provide information children need to complete tasks themselves.
  - Support and encourage alternative techniques.

REFERENCES

American Foundation for the Blind (n.d.). Transition happens, ready or not! Retrieved from http://www.afb.org/info/for-family-and-friends/transition/35.

Bowen, J. (2010). Visual impairment and its impact on self-esteem: What makes a difference. *British Journal of Visual Impairment, 28*(3): 235–243.

Cameto, R. & Nagle, K. (2007). *Facts from NLTS2: Orientation and mobility skills of secondary school students with visual impairments* (NCSET 2008-2007). Washington, DC: National Center for Special Education Research. Retrieved from: https://ies.ed.gov/pubsearch/pubsinfo.asp?pubid=NCSER20083007.

Castellano, C. (1991). Tips for classroom teachers. *Future Reflections, 10*(3). Retrieved from http://www.blindchildren.org/textonly/to_edu_dev/3_5_4.html.

Cutter, J. (1997). Valuing the blind child's independent movements and travel. *Braille Monitor*, *40*(5). Retrieved from https://nfb.org/images/nfb/publications/bm/bm97/bm970505.htm.

9

TRIALS AND TRIBULATIONS

Many people have referred to puberty as an awkward stage of human development, often stating that it is one period of life they would never want to repeat. Others simply associate this period of life with growing pains. Nonetheless, it is a trying time in the life of young people.

To make things worse, most students experience puberty at the same time as they are faced with one of the most challenging educational transitions: the move from elementary school into middle school. Vernon (1993) points out that this is an especially difficult time for young females as they struggle with the onset of puberty, a period of growth and development marked by a roller-coaster of hormonal and physical changes. Interestingly, many of their same-age male counterparts tend to fare better during this period of development, as males are often praised for manly attributes and characteristics such as athleticism, facial hair, and muscle development.

VIGNETTE

Rachael always persevered through life's setbacks. Her parents divorced at about the time she entered school, an older sibling was killed in a car wreck when she was in second grade, and her mother moved back east around the time she entered the intermediate grades.

She was an average to above-average student, though she had been retained in kindergarten because of her inability to stay focused in class. The next year she was diagnosed with ADHD and placed on medication by her family doctor. She remained on meds throughout her years in elementary school. Over time, she developed the skills needed to succeed in the classroom, and she performed at benchmark by the time she transitioned to middle school.

Rachael lived with her father and paternal grandmother after her parents' divorce until she started middle school. It was this point that she moved to Kentucky to live with her mother and her stepfather. After moving to her mother's home, Rachael spent most of the summer at home alone. She had no friends or peers in her neighborhood and longed for someone her age to hang out with. Making new friends always seemed difficult for her, causing her to often wonder what was it that was so different about her. For Rachael, moving to another state and starting a new school where she knew nobody was worrisome, to say the least.

By the time Rachael began middle school that fall her body had gone through a metamorphosis. She had begun to mature physically; she had gained weight and grew three inches seemingly overnight, becoming a buxom thirteen-year-old girl. Rachael was uneasy with this noticeable change in her appearance. She tried to hide her adult figure by wearing loose-fitting, baggy clothing.

Rachael hated her body and was terribly self-conscious about her mature features. She wore dark makeup, dyed her hair black, and had piercings on her face—one in her eyebrow and a smaller stud in her nostril—all to distract attention from her upper torso.

On more than one occasion she reported to the principal inappropriate comments pertaining to her figure made by some of the boys in her class. This frustrated Rachael greatly and only added to the difficulties of her transition. Though the staff was put on alert by the principal to watch for harassing comments, many students continued to poke fun at her, and she felt uncomfortable at school. Her attendance began to suffer, as did her grades.

What can schools and educators intentionally do to help students achieve a better acceptance and respect of their developing bodies?

RESEARCH

For preadolescent girls, the hormonal and physical changes they are experiencing, combined with their efforts to maintain a positive self-image, are nearly overwhelming. Vernon (1993) studied the impact of these changes and how they affect adolescent and preadolescent females as they transition to middle school. Because the rate at which adolescents enter puberty varies, there exists no preset timetable. For many young females the onset of puberty also brings about their first menstrual period as well as changes in physical appearance such as weight gain and the development of breasts.

Akos, Queen, and Lineberry (2005) suggest that "early adolescents require time and energy to get accustomed to their new bodies" (p. 19). The changes adolescents face during the awkward stage of puberty often have a negative impact on self-esteem as they attempt to maintain a positive self-image under what feels like constant scrutiny about their appearance by their peers.

Further complicating the emotional roller-coaster associated with this period in a young girl's life, during this time their innate need for acceptance from their peer group begins to include members of the opposite sex. This is also a time when adolescents often face issues such as sexual harassment. An American Association of University Women survey of 1,965 students in grades seven through twelve found that 48 percent of students reported experiencing some kind of sexual harassment during the 2010–2011 school year.

The AAUW study further discovered that "[g]irls were more likely than boys to be sexually harassed by a significant margin (56 percent versus 40 percent). Girls were also more likely than boys to be sexually harassed both in person (52 percent versus 35 percent) and via electronic means [text, e-mail, Facebook, or other electronic media] (36 percent versus 24 percent)" (GoLocalProv Health, 2011).

INTERVENTION

Preadolescent students are often overly concerned about what peers think and how they are viewed by others. Unfortunately, our society often encourages adolescent females to seek acceptance through their physical appearance (Akos, Queen, & Lineberry, 2005). It is during this same period that the onset of puberty—associated with physical growth and hormonal change and often linked with periods of depression, feelings of despair, and constant self-evaluation—occurs.

The support and assistance of parents and teachers is even more important during this period of life, as the issues of making friends, dealing with harassment, and fitting in are paramount for many students. Schools must have systems of support and intentionally developed transition activities in place that further inform teachers and students about procedures for reporting harassment and teaching coping skills.

Strategies and Suggestions

The following intervention strategies for parents are adapted from GoLocalProv Health (2011).

- Communicate with your child.
- Encourage your child to confide in you about issues pertaining to harassment and bullying.
- Assure your child that you will not ban electronic devices if he or she shares offensive language or behavior experienced from others online.
- Contact your child's teachers and principal.
- Establish expectations for peer-to-peer interactions.

- Listen carefully to your child.
- Determine what happened and who was involved.
- Don't assume you child did something to warrant this behavior.
- Never tell the child to ignore harassing behavior.
- Never encourage retaliation.
- Speak with the school administration.
- Contact the police or a lawyer.
- Know what devices and electronic media your child utilizes.
- Talk to your child about privacy and self-protection
- Review the school's digital user agreements and policies on cyberbullying and harassment, and discuss any examples of inappropriate content provided.
- Broaden your understanding of cyberbulling using Internet resources:

    - www.stopbullyingri.com
    - www.commonsensemedia.org
    - www.netsmartz.org
    - www.cyberbullying.us

REFERENCES

Akos, P., Queen, J.A., & Lineberry, C. (2005). *Promoting a successful transition to middle school.* Larchmont, NY: Routledge.

GoLocalProvHealth. (2011). Sexual harassment in middle school on the rise. Retrieved from http://www.golocalprov.com/health/sexual-harassment-in-middle-school-on-the-rise.

Vernon, A. (1993). *Developmental assessment and intervention with children and adolescents.* Alexandria, VA: American Counseling Association.

10

WORDS CAN'T EXPRESS

Many of us take for granted such simple things as the ability to have a conversation with a peer or casual acquaintance. For most of us, speaking and communicating occurs in our daily lives with very little effort—unless, of course, you are talking about public speaking, which is in a category all its own. But as for the day-to-day communications necessary in life, most people seldom give it a second thought.

Now imagine the difficulty individuals who stutter have with this same communication process. For students who stutter, something as simple as answering a question or reading a passage from the book can be a major feat.

Millions of Americans suffer with the speech issue known as stuttering. Though the exact causes of stuttering for the most part are unknown, researchers acknowledge that nearly 60 percent of individuals with these symptoms have a relative with the same problem, leading many to believe that it may be hereditary. Others speculate that anxiety and nervousness may cause many of the symptoms related to stuttering.

Many children develop repetitive speech patterns and stuttering between the ages of two and five years old. Though most children to outgrow these symptoms, many do not, continuing to stutter into adulthood. Others are able to overcome their symptoms with the help of specialized speech training from speech and language pathologists.

VIGNETTE

Johnny Ray was always been described by his teachers as a delightful young man who was always very compassionate toward his peers. He was very studious and eager to please his teachers. Johnny Ray was much like any other twelve-year-old boy, with the exception of his speech problem: he suffered from problematic stuttering, experiencing increased difficulty during times of stress or anxiety. Johnny Ray participated in speech class beginning in early elementary school, but although he made marked improvement over the years, as he entered middle school he still had a persistent stutter.

As Johnny Ray moved through the primary and intermediate grades, his peers were very accepting of him, paying little notice to his stutter. He was well liked and always included in peer activities, including basketball. Johnny Ray loved basketball and was quite impressive on the court, breaking his school's record for free-throw percentage during his last year in grade school. Johnny Ray loved school and being around his peers. He seldom ever missed school; he was one of the top students in his fifth-grade class and had always been on the honor role.

When Johnny Ray transitioned to middle school, he experienced a few run-ins with some of the other students, who mocked him and made fun of his stutter. This angered Johnny immensely, and he lashed out at his aggressors. On more than one occasion this seemingly delightful boy had ended up in in-school suspension (ISS) for fighting. Johnny Ray didn't think it was fair that he was punished for defending himself, even though his principal had explained the school's zero-tolerance policy, which required ISS for anyone engaged in a physical confrontation.

Johnny Ray's father also strongly disagreed with his son's punishment. He made clear—to both the principal and the district superintendent—his expectation that the harassing behavior would stop and demanded that the school ensure the other students did not mock or make fun of his son.

Johnny Ray hated the entire situation, often arguing with his dad that he could handle it, though his father knew better: No student should be picked on or belittled by others. Eventually Johnny Ray began to withdraw from his peer group, and for the first time he began to dread going to school. He increasingly kept to himself and avoided conversations with peers. His interest in extracurricular activities such as basketball also began to dwindle. Though he managed to keep his grades up, the social aspect of middle school life began to wear heavily on this once-outgoing student.

Johnny Ray's only wish was that he could somehow stop his stuttering so that he would fit in with the rest of the group. He hated his condition and often pondered what life would be like if he could only communicate fluently.

Johnny Ray needed intervention. Luckily, the middle school boys' basketball coach, Coach Stevens, and Johnny Ray's father continued to encourage him to try out for the basketball team. Mr. Smith, the middle school counselor, and Coach Stevens began to mentor Johnny Ray and convinced the principal to begin a school-wide campaign against bullying and harassment. Johnny Ray also continued speech training under the direction of a new speech pathologist assigned to the middle school.

Johnny Ray's speech teacher was Mrs. Krieger, a brilliant lady who greatly enjoyed working with children. Under her persistent guidance, Johnny Ray's speech problem continued to improve. She always stressed to him the importance of taking his time while speaking and encouraged him to block out the anxious feelings that often haunted him while speaking. She spent countless hours working with and assisting Johnny Ray, and she was determined to stay abreast of new treatments and interventions for stuttering. Her determination and perseverance made a difference: as the year progressed, so did Johnny Ray's outlook.

RESEARCH

Büchel and Sommer (2004) classify stuttering in one of two categories: persistent developmental stuttering (PDS) and neurogenic, or acquired, stuttering, which is typically caused by some form of damage to the brain due to injury such as blunt force trauma or stroke. According to their findings, PDS first appears in most children between the ages of two and five. PDS is the more common form of stuttering found in adolescents; Büchel and Sommer estimate that nearly 3 million people in the United States suffer from PDS.

It is important to note that the research clearly indicates that these symptoms persist equally in all demographics, with no social class or race presenting a higher rate of occurrence (Bushel & Sommer, 2004), although the American Speech-Language-Hearing Association (ASHA, 2013) does report that males are three to four times more likely to develop stuttering than females.

ASHA (2013) also reports,

> The development of stuttering varies considerably across individuals. Some children show significant difficulty with speech fluency within days or weeks of onset. Others show a gradual increase in fluency difficulties over months or years. Furthermore, the severity of children's stuttering can vary greatly from day to day and week to week. With some children, the disfluencies may appear to go away for several weeks, only to start again for no apparent reason. For teens and young adults who stutter, the symptoms of stuttering tend to be more stable than they are during early childhood. Still, teen and adult speakers may report that their speech fluency is significantly better or worse than usual during specific activities.

Research indicates that nearly 75 percent of children who stutter will eventually experience cessation of symptoms; some simply outgrow the symptoms, while others improve with the aid of intervention from certified speech and language pathologists (ASHA, 2013). Other research also supports the notion that stuttering will stop on its own, though in some preadolescent children the symptoms persist much longer (KidsHealth, 2013).

Many children who stutter are teased by their peers. This in turn leads to an increase in anxiety and can have negative impact on self-esteem (KidsHealth, 2013). In some adolescent children the fear or anxiety experienced from stuttering can even perpetuate the symptoms, causing the condition to continue or even worsen (Duckworth, 2004).

INTERVENTIONS

Students who stutter seek to free themselves from their speech disabilities so they will not be harassed or teased about it by other children. They want to live without fear of stuttering. All they want is to fit in and not be ostracized from their peer groups. Often they began to resent their speech problems and consider it the source of their unhappiness.

As their self-esteem suffers, these students often withdraw from interaction with their peer groups. They need intervention. Schools can help these students by providing transition activities that teach students tolerance of others, how to report incidences of unacceptable behavior, and how to include students with disabilities in regular school activities.

Strategies and Suggestions

For teachers:

- Don't tell the child to "slow down" or "just relax."
- Don't complete words or sentences for the child.
- Develop classroom routines that encourage all students to take turns speaking and listening. Children who stutter find it easier to speak when there are fewer interruptions.

- Hold all students to the same high expectations. Expect the same quality and quantity of work from students who stutter.
- Communicate with the student in an unhurried way, pausing frequently.
- Never make stuttering something the student is ashamed of. Talk about the symptoms just like any other matter.
- Discuss needed accommodations in the classroom with the child, but do not be an enabler. (Scott, 2012)

For parents:

- Don't require your child to speak precisely or correctly at all times. Allow talking to be fun and enjoyable.
- Use family meals as a conversation time. Avoid distractions such as radio or TV.
- Avoid corrections or criticisms such as "slow down," "take your time," or "take a deep breath." These comments, however well-intentioned, will only make your child feel more self-conscious.
- Avoid having your child speak or read aloud when uncomfortable or when the stuttering increases. Instead, during these times encourage activities that do not require a lot of talking.
- Don't interrupt your child or tell him or her to start over.
- Don't tell your child to think before speaking.
- Provide a calm atmosphere in the home. Try to slow down the pace of family life.
- Speak slowly and clearly when talking to your child or others in his or her presence.
- Maintain natural eye contact with your child. Try not to look away or show signs of being upset.
- Let your child speak for him- or herself and to finish thoughts and sentences. Pause before responding to your child's questions or comments.
- Talk slowly to your child. This takes practice! Modeling a slow rate of speech will help with your child's fluency. (Nelson, 2010)

REFERENCES

American Speech-Language-Hearing Association (2013) Stuttering. Retrieved from http://www.asha.org/public/speech/disorders/stuttering.htm.

Büchel, C. & Sommer, M. (2004). What causes stuttering? *PLoS Biology 2*(2), 159–163.

Duckworth, D. (2004). *Causes and treatment of stuttering in young children*. Greenville, SC: Super Duper Publications. Retrieved from https://www.google.com/url?sa=t&rct=j&q=&esrc=s&source=web&cd=1&cad=rja&uact=8&ved=0ahUKEwjppIuO_trZAhUEpFkKHc01AFQQFgguMAA&url=https%3A%2F%2Fwww.superduperinc.com%2Fhandouts%2Fpdf%2F65_Cause_and_Treatment_of%2520Stuttering.pdf&usg=AOvVaw1SR6_nmyv9ZmpO4iTcnln6.

KidsHealth. (2013). Stuttering. Retrieved from http://kidshealth.org/parent/emotions/behavior/stutter.html.

Nelson, A. (2010). What parents can do. Retrieved from http://kidshealth.org/parent/emotions/behavior/stutter.html

Scott, L.A. (2012). 8 tips for teachers. In *The child who stutters at school: Notes to the teacher*. Memphis, TN: Stuttering Foundation. Retrieved from http://www.stutteringhelp.org/sites/default/files/Migrate/0042NT.pdf.

11

SLACKER

Nearly every middle school teacher can identify at least one student who just never performed to his or her ability level. When teachers receive their rosters each year, they review assessment scores, grades, and benchmark performance ratings of their students. It is always disappointing to a teacher when a child simply does not achieve at the level they have in the past or to which they are capable.

Often there are underlying reasons for this. The causes often vary from events pertaining to their home life (such as relocation, divorce, etc.) to physiological and biological factors associated with the onset of puberty, transitioning from one level of school to the next, and change in general.

Whatever the reason, the more familiar teachers are with their respective students and their individual needs, the better able they are to develop action plans to help their kids. Connecting with students before they show up for class is one way of ensuring student success. As Lorain (2011) notes, the most significant step to ensuring a "successful middle school experience" is the transition plan.

Some schools go to rather extensive ends to connect with and assist students during transitions by preparing formal transition plans that encompass the physical, emotional, academic, and social needs of the students. Schools that utilize formal transition plans involving all stakeholders during this most challenging stage of adolescence experience fewer issues that negatively impact student outcomes (Lorain, 2011).

VIGNETTE

Timmy was a very bright young man who had always excelled in academics and sports. He was the middle child in his family, and his siblings were both high achievers. His older brother was in high school and very popular with his peers. His younger sister, still in elementary school, seemed to excel at everything. In elementary school, Timmy was in the top 10 percent of his class and was self-motivated; it was as if he was driven to be the best in everything he participated in. It was no surprise that he was identified for the gifted and talented program during the fourth grade.

His parents were well-educated and successful professionals with a very strong work ethic, and they always stressed the importance of hard work and maintaining good grades to their children. Upon transition to middle school, Timmy regressed, becoming an average student. He quit all his extracurricular activities, using the excuse that they were interfering with his academics and that he did not have time to study—even though he seldom brought home any assignments and rarely studied for tests. He no longer was driven to be the *best* student.

At home, Timmy began testing the rules and boundaries. He started questioning authority and talking back to his parents. He frequently became very emotional and had difficulty controlling his outbursts. His interactions with his siblings were often very negative, many times ending in an argument. Timmy also became very involved in video games and spent most of his free time at home on the Xbox.

Physically, Timmy was in the prepubescent phase of adolescence, with the associated weight gain and mild acne. He was becoming increasingly concerned about his physical appearance, particularly his weight. His parents continued to encourage him to participate in athletics, knowing that this would help keep him physically fit. Unfortunately, Timmy had joined the sixth-grade football team after school started, so he missed most of summer conditioning. Lagging far behind, he eventually quit the team during the second month of practice.

The one thing he did enjoy at school was the Yearbook Club, but when one of the teachers he admired did not choose him to help with the fun task of going to local businesses to sell yearbook advertisements, he became very upset. When he asked his teacher why he was not chosen, the response he received was both inappropriate and demoralizing: he was told he was not selected because he was not one of the teacher's favorite students.

This was such a disappointment to Timmy that he lost respect for all of his teachers and essentially gave up on middle school altogether. Though his parents were intent on Timmy making good grades and achieving, it was a struggle just to get him to school every day. He spent the majority of his sixth grade year grounded, with most of his personal effects and privileges taken away.

Are we aware of the changes happening within our students? When a once active and engaged student no longer participates in extracurricular activities, this signals the need for intervention. What is the root cause of this withdrawal? What can educators do to help students like Timmy who are becoming more lost in the transition?

RESEARCH

It is extremely important that teachers and parents remember that the preadolescent child who is now contending with moodiness, anxiety, irresponsible behavior, and lifelessness is the same child as the once passive, upbeat, and loveable student who seemed to perform almost effortlessly in the elementary grades. The reality of this stage of development is that preadolescent children will exhibit robust energy at one moment and near lifelessness the next (Baenen, 2005).

Though parents and teachers tend to find this package deal very difficult to handle at times, they should persevere through this transition in their child's life. Research and understanding will lead to patience and tolerance of the behaviors of the adolescent child. Better understanding this stage of development will also provide effective strategies in dealing with lethargic behavior and emotional outbursts.

There is no set time frame for the emergence of adolescence. Most children tend to show the physical changes associated with puberty—which causes the adrenal glands to produce hormones known as *adrenal androgens*—between the ages of eight and fourteen (KidsHealth, 2013). The notable effects for boys are the development of facial hair, testosterone production, and deepening of the voice; effects for girls include the development of breast tissue, the onset of menstruation, and the production of estrogen.

There is a distinction between puberty and adolescence, but the two impact the growing child simultaneously (KidsHealth, 2013). Unlike puberty, the adolescent period of development, is associated with very little physical change. Instead, adolescence is marked by biological and emotional changes influencing the desire to seek independence from their parents and to discover their own identity (American Academy of Child & Adolescent Psychiatry, 2016).

Behaviors common in the adolescent stage of development are often interpreted as being disrespectful or inappropriate. These include mood swings, lack of interest in previously enjoyed activities, the tendency to exhibit childish behavior when stressed, impulsive decision making, and even dangerous or risky actions (American Academy of Child & Asolescent Psychiatry, 2016).

INTERVENTIONS

Parents must endeavor to remain connected with their children as they enter the preadolescent stage of development. Persistence and compassion, combined with effective role modeling and communication skills, are crucial. It is common for preadolescents to attempt to shut out their parents, but in reality they need their parents at this stage more than ever before (KidsHealth, 2013).

It is during this stage of development that children become more preoccupied with their peer groups; this is normal behavior. Parents sometimes feel as though their involvement and interaction with their children have been "traded in" for that of their peer group (KidsHealth, 2013), but in fact preadolescents are merely expanding and growing as they seek out their own identities and independence. This is a part of the nature of human growth and development.

Strategies and Suggestions

For teachers:

- Mentor the students who are showing increasing difficulty fitting in.
- Research and review the adolescent stage of development. Identify with your students. Focus on the Middle School Concept.
- Communicate with your students.
- Participate in character education classes with the students. Include these in the curriculum where appropriate.
- Provide as much choice as possible in assignments and homework. Allowing children to make decisions will help them develop autonomy.

For parents:

Retrieved from www.KidsHealth.org.

- Create special time with the family. Ensure that all your children participate.
- Plan family meal time. Schedule this in advance and include children in conversation.
- Show affection. Tell your children you love them frequently—then show them.

- Share one-on-one time with your preteen. Enjoy each other's company. Communicate but don't argue. Be willing to listen more than advising.

REFERENCES

American Academy of Child & Adolescent Psychiatry. (2016). Teen brain: Behavior, problem solving, and decision making. *Facts for Families, 95*. Retrieved from https://www.aacap.org/AACAP/Families_and_Youth/Facts_for_Families/FFF-Guide/The-Teen-Brain-Behavior-Problem-Solving-and-Decision-Making-095.aspx

Baenen, J. (2005). *H.E.L.P.: How to enjoy living with a preadolescent*. Westerville, OH: National Middle School Association.

KidsHealth. (2013). A parent's guide to surviving the teen years. Retrieved from http://kidshealth.org/parent/growth/growing/adolescence.html

Lorain, P. (2011). Transition to middle school. Retrieved from http://www.nea.org/tools/16657.htm.

12

SOCIAL IMMATURITY

There exists a wide spectrum of emotional maturity among adolescent male children, with attention-seeking behavior often indicating immaturity. Students lacking the social or emotional maturity of their peer group often resort to foolishness to gain the attention of the crowd. This behavior frequently lands them in the principal's office and has a tendency to aggravate even the most patient bystander.

VIGNETTE

"All right, young man—you just earned yourself a detention," said Mrs. Stephens sternly.

"But all I did was ask her if she ever played Suck and Blow," replied Tommy.

"You will report to the principal's office!" shouted Mrs. Stephens, with her finger pointed toward the classroom door. "I will not have that kind of talk in my classroom."

As Tommy rose from his desk with a smirky grin, he slowly looked over his shoulder to observe his peers reaction, replying, "But it is only a card game." As he walked toward the door he noticed the snickering of some of the boys in his class.

Tommy's attitude and behavior were not uncommon as of late. In the month since school started, he had already served several detentions and two separate office visits for unruly or disruptive behavior. He was certain this time he would be placed in in-school suspension—or even suspended. As he began to worry about his parents' reaction, Tommy shuddered to think of being grounded for the rest of his life. As he slowly approached Mr. Whit's office, he quickly began to mentally rehearse his plea in the hopes of avoiding punishment.

Though Tommy wasn't truly a bad egg, his immature behavior was creating quite a disturbance at school. He had always been a top student and was described by his former teachers as one of the brightest they ever had in class. When Tommy entered the early primary grades, he thrilled his teachers with his inquisitiveness and his ability to easily comprehend material. He was the first among his peers to begin reading, and boy, did he read. His first grade teacher, Mrs. Brewer, frequently took him to read to the principal and other staff members in his school.

By the time Tommy finished first grade, his teachers were encouraging his parents and the school administration to allow him to enter third grade in the fall instead of attending second grade with his peers, essentially double promoting him. His teachers were certain that with his physical size and intelligence he would adjust quickly. His mother was concerned that he would not fit in socially with the older group of children, though the teachers assured her he would be fine.

As Tommy continued through elementary school, his progress seemed to slow as he found himself trying to fit in with the older crowd instead of focusing his attention on learning. Though his grades never really suffered, he no longer achieved at the accelerated rate of his earlier years.

Because of his late birthday, Tommy was nearly a year and a half younger than the rest of his class. He was where he needed to be academically, but socially he was immature, a problem compounded because he was so much younger than the others. The impact of his age did not really begin to surface until he transitioned to middle school, where he found himself seeking attention from a much larger audience of peers, often leading to attention-seeking and annoying behavior.

As Tommy entered the preadolescent stage of his development, he found himself fighting an uphill battle, with much of his attention now focused on members of the opposite sex. Tommy had apparently gone "girl crazy," as his mother once remarked. His immaturity and inappropriate remarks had the tendency to repel girls rather than impress them.

This was a very trying time for Tommy at home as well. He found it increasingly harder to communicate with his parents, especially about issues at school. He seemed to be spending more time in his room on the computer communicating with his friends or outside playing basketball in the driveway. Tommy's younger brother was often the target of his rude comments and putdowns, as the age difference between the two boys made it difficult for him to connect with and relate to his own sibling. At home he withdrew to his room, while at school he became the class clown, acting out as a means of trying to fit in.

Educators need to take notice of the difficulties faced by students at varying maturity levels and work collaboratively to design transition activities to help students to interact with their peers in a positive manner. Part of the role of teachers includes guiding students to interact socially in appropriate ways; this is often referred to as the *hidden curriculum.*

When students are double promoted to higher grades or to advanced honors classes, is there a plan in place to monitor these moves? Do educators have a transition plan to integrate advanced kids into classes at higher grade levels, where cliques and groups are already formed? Acting out is a reaction to the need for attention. In these situations, educators should ask themselves why the student is reacting in this manner and what kind of attention is needed to navigate this transition. Behaviors such as this, if left unattended by adults, may not produce the desired results for the student.

Adolescence is a period of rapid changes. Between the ages of 12 and 17, for example, a parent ages as much as 20 years.—Author Unknown

RESEARCH

The preadolescent years are a time of rapid growth for the developing brain of the child (Chamberlain, 2009). One of the last regions of the brain to develop in adolescent males is the prefrontal cortex, the control center for regulating impulsive behavior, problem solving, and rational thought processes. Chamberlain asserts that due to the development of the adolescent brain, younger teenagers may actually not be entirely at fault when it comes to poor decision making, moodiness, and impulsive behaviors. Understanding the physical development of the adolescent brain assists both parents and educators in understanding why children sometimes act like *children*: They are not adults and do not have the full benefit of mature brain functions.

Abrams (2011) argues that boys and girls differ greatly in both physical and emotional maturity:

> Boys are not just different from girls, but also in many ways more vulnerable. Boys are born six weeks behind girls developmentally, a gap that widens throughout childhood right up to puberty, by which time they are two years behind. In infancy, boys cry more, take longer to settle, and are slower to learn to walk, talk and potty train. They have more difficulty adapting to school. Reading, writing, sitting still all come harder to small boys. Socially, too, they lag behind girls. Behavioral problems and mental illnesses, from autism to attention deficit disorder, are more common at all ages in boys than girls. In adolescence boys do less well at school, leave school earlier, and are more likely than girls to die, in road accidents, from substance abuse, in fights and by suicide.

Chamberlain (2009) notes that although the adolescent period of development is a time when children are seeking independence and personal identity, it is also a time when they most need to spend quality time with parents and other well-adjusted adults to assist in shaping their developing brains by mentoring and modeling effective actions and behavior.

INTERVENTIONS

For many, adolescence is a period marked by separation from the parent and increased connection to the peer group. This period in social development often leads to status-seeking, often risky or even dangerous behavior, along with rebellious behavior such as nonperformance (Chamberlain, 2009).

Child psychologists and researchers agree that the preadolescent stage of development is often a very troublesome time for children (Chamberlin, 2009; Abrams, 2011). It is during this stage of development that educators and parents must be mindful of many of the stressors, including physical and emotional changes, that face preadolescent children, striving to establish effective and age-appropriate interventions to assist them during this phase of life.

Strategies and Suggestions

For teachers:

- Remember each child is an individual:

    - Don't expect all children to act and behave the same way.
    - Post classroom rules and expectations.
    - Teach the expected behaviors and rehearse them frequently with students.
    - Never assume that all students fully understand.

- Deal with discipline without embarrassing children, and praise appropriate behavior and recognize effort; this builds self-esteem (Dweck, 2008).
- Find the time to work one-on-one with immature students, teaching proper interactions for conversation and communication and providing opportunities for students to rehearse in small groups.
- Encourage your school to adopt a character education program such as Second Steps, a nationally recognized program that teaches an effective character education curriculum with focus on socialization behaviors (Second Step, 2012).
- Develop an adult mentor program to assist with the development.

For parents:

Retrieved from: http://communities.washingtontimes.com/neighborhood/loris-centiments/2012/jan/8/teenage-boys-sweet-sons-narcissistic-teens/

- Get involved with your adolescent. Spend quality time together.
- Mentor and role model proper behavior for your child.
- Discuss and role-play everyday situations pertaining to social interaction.
- Encourage extracurricular activities that foster positive social interactions with others.
- Learn to listen to your child. Do not attempt to do all the talking; listening is key to effective communication.
- Limit video game play on the Xbox and television viewing to reasonable time periods.
- Teach organizational skills by creating schedules and structure at home.
- Establish routines such as mealtime and lights out. Discuss the importance of sleep for the adolescent brain development and ensure plenty of rest, but allow your child to have input on this decision rather than dictating it to them.

REFERENCES

Abrams, R. (2011, August 18). In praise of sons. *Psychologies*. Retrieved from http://psychologies.co.uk/family/sons-be-praised.html

Chamberlain, L.B. (2009). The amazing teen brain: What every child advocate needs to know. *Child Law Practice, 28*(2). Retrieved from http://www.childandanimalaw.com/wp-content/uploads/2012/02/The-Amazing-Teen-Brain.pdf.

Dweck, C. S. (2008). The perils of promises and praise. *The Best of Educational Leadership 2007–2008, 65*, 34–39.

Second Step (2012). www.SecondStep.org.

ABOUT THE AUTHORS

C. Thomas Potter II, EdD, has served the education profession as a teacher, principal, and superintendent in Kentucky for more than twenty-two years. He is one of twenty-five superintendents selected to serve in a leadership cohort sponsored by the National Institute of School Leaders. He holds a master of arts in secondary education and a doctorate in educational administration from Morehead State University.

Kevin S. Koett, EdD, has served as a mentor, instructor, and student affairs professional in higher education for more than twenty-eight years. He has served in a variety of roles at six different institutions and has been recognized for his servant-leadership as the first recipient of the Joe Buck Service Award. He holds a bachelor of arts in social studies teaching from Augustana College, a master of science in higher education administration from Syracuse University, and a doctorate in educational leadership from Morehead State University.

Carol Christian, EdD, has served as a teacher, coach, principal, and professor in Kentucky for more than thirty years. She is a coauthor of *Privileged Thinking in Today's Schools: The Implications of Social Justice and Heart to Heart* (2010). She was selected to serve in Kentucky's Highly Skilled Educator Program, working with low-performing schools. She holds degrees from Eastern Kentucky University and a doctorate in education from the University of Louisville.

www.ingramcontent.com/pod-product-compliance
Lightning Source LLC
Chambersburg PA
CBHW032030230426
43671CB00005B/266